NERDY EVER AFTER

Confessions of a Nerdy Girl

A Nerdy Novel, Book 1

By Linda Rey

Pretty Bird Literary
28421 Mission Viejo, CA 92692

ISBN: 978-0-9993120-5-6

Cover art by www.fiverr.com/Nizar86

Suggested ages: 9 -14
Summary: A self-professed nerdy girl uses the popularity of the hottest guy in school to bring acceptance to a new classmate — a boy with cerebral palsy who sits in a wheelchair.

*Note to parents, readers, and educators: The *Confessions of a Nerdy Girl* novel series strives to showcase diverse characters and experiences. Storylines may include (but are not limited to) the following subjects: adoption, divorce, ethnic and cultural minorities, people with disabilities, homelessness, OCD, ADHD, LGBT+ and gender identity.

Pssst… Willa has a secret. Actually, she has lots of them, and she's put them all in her very first diary, *Confessions of a Nerdy Girl: TOP SECRET*. Sign up for **NERDY NEWS** to get notifications on how to get the book for FREE, and you'll also receive a gift of Nerdy Wordz, a fun word game to play by yourself, or with friends. Sign up today! www.subscribepage.com/nerdywordz

This book is dedicated to every girl who, like me, has more books than friends, and is totally okay with it.

Table of Contents

CHAPTER 1

"Hey, twerp." Blaine flicked her blonde ponytail and then shook a blue and white pom-pom in my face.

Following her lead, my adoptive sister, Olivia, copied her friend, ponytail toss and all. "Yeah, what's up, dork?"

I rolled my eyes at them and stepped aside to let them pass me in the hallway.

According to my lab experiment in Mr. Bennett's science class, between the two of them there wasn't enough brainpower to illuminate a single light bulb. Not a standard one, either. I'm talking 4-watt night-light.

And what was up with the twerp and the dork?

"Watching those *Mean Girls* reruns again, have you, ladies?" I joked, pushing my glasses tighter against my nose and raising my eyebrows.

"Who you calling *ladies*?" Olivia snapped. "And it was *Pretty Little Liars*, not *Mean Girls*, weirdo. *Mean Girls* is so a hundred years ago."

"Actually, the movie premiered April 30, 2004. You're off by over a decade."

"See what I mean?" Olivia looked at Blaine and shook her head in disgust. "Could she be any weirder? I can't believe my parents adopted her. Honestly, Blaine, you have no idea what it's like to live with an artistic savant."

I rolled my eyes skyward before settling them on Olivia's perfect face. "First, the word you're looking for is *autistic*, not artistic, and second, 'savant' is pronounced like want, and not like ant or pant."

"Who *cares*?" She roughly brushed my shoulder, and the two crossed the threshold into Olivia's den of darkness, slamming the door behind them.

"Is she really autistic?" I heard Blaine say. "She looks normal-ish."

I didn't hear Olivia's answer because by then I was halfway down the hallway.

Despite what Olivia said, I'm not an autistic savant, which the dictionary defines as a person affected with a mental disability who shows exceptional skills in mathematics or music. As a matter of fact, I pretty much suck at both math and music. Unless, of course, we're referring to my ability to *listen* to music. In which case I do okay.

But it's not as though I'm normal, either.

Medical books list me as "MS." It's short for "Minor Shisbey," and I'm number thirteen. Make that *unlucky* thirteen. I'm the thirteenth documented person in the world to have something called H-SAM, Highly Superior Auto Biographical Memory. I'm also the last documented case, unless someone else has come out of the H-SAM closet that I don't know about.

Having H-SAM doesn't make me a genius or anything, and it doesn't give me a photographic memory. It just means I can recall any information personally linked to me. The things I saw or heard. How things smelled, or the way I felt.

Not that there's anything super fantastic to tell so far. At thirteen, I think I'm stuck in a commercial break and all the good stuff must happen in the second half of the show.

I can recall, with complete accuracy, all the memories of my life, stored in my brain like information on a computer hard drive and with the ability to retrieve them in an instant whether I want to or not. Not my actual birth, of course, that would be a stretch, not to mention gross, but beginning the day after my first birthday when my birth mom held me in her arms and knocked on the door of the Children's Home Society of Chicago, crying to the woman who answered that she just couldn't keep me anymore.

You probably think I'm famous for being number thirteen, but I'm not. At least not in the real world. You won't see me on talk shows like *Good Morning* … (insert city here), or *Good Day* … (same thing). Unless you're one of the doctors at the Department of Neurology at the University of California, who tested me and knew my real name—correction, my *adopted* name, because I don't know my real last name—I'll go down in history as just MS.

My full name is Wilhelmina Eugenia Shisbey, (I know, right? Could it be any worse?) but people call me Willa. My records are sealed, so I don't know much about my birth parents, but I'm told my mother named me after Wilhelmina Cooper, the famous model who started one of the top modeling agencies in New York City back in the 60s. Maybe it's a lie, or maybe it's not.

I'd like to think it's the truth. That sometime before I was born, before my mother saw her hopes dashed the minute she saw me—a homely kid with a cleft lip and a wonky eye—that she had big dreams for me. I still don't know where the Eugenia came from, but I do know I'd love to send it back from wherever it was. (Like 258 AD, the last time the name was popular.) Shisbey I inherited four years later, when my adoption became final after my dad, Ted Shisbey, who had been my dentist at the orphanage, and his wife, Diane, took me into their home.

A home that unfortunately also included their eight-year-old biological daughter, Olivia. To say Olivia has hated me from the start would not be an exaggeration, and eight years later things are definitely NOT improving.

The door to Olivia's room swung open and Olivia stuck her head out. In the reflection of the mirrored closet doors I saw Blaine practicing cheer moves between selfie shots.

"Oh, I forgot to tell you," Olivia blew a bubble with her gum and let it pop before finishing, "your little friend is outside. She wanted to know if you could come out and *play*."

Both Dumb and Dumber thought the line was pure gold and collapsed into a fit of giggles.

Marley Applegate is my new best friend and she has a dry sense of humor most people don't get. (Her "come out and play" line was a joke, Olivia. Duh!) I met Marley the first day I attended school in California after moving from Lincoln Park, a suburb in Chicago. It was May 16th, a Thursday, and just three weeks before the end of the school year.

Diane and Olivia had already been here for a couple of weeks so Olivia could qualify for the cheer team at Huntington Harbor. Dad and I stayed behind while he tied up the loose ends with his dental practice and worked out the details of his new partnership. I had two weeks without Olivia … or her mom, (who I will never consider *my* mom). It was just Dad and me. Pure bliss.

The day I met Marley she came up to me at the Friendship Bench where I sat, alone, eating my lunch. In case you haven't heard of it, the Friendship Bench is the place where all the nerds go to find another nerd to befriend. Once successfully paired, you're required to pay it forward and return to the bench to introduce yourself to the next student too shy or uncool to meet people without the aid of a hookup point. The hope is eventually all the nerds and the misfits in the school will have met.

Think of the Friendship Bench as the Match dot com of the geeks and the socially awkward.

Marley is half-black, small for her age, and super smart. She has some crazy-high IQ and is the editor of the school paper. Marley is the only person I know who hates her name almost as much as I hate mine. But if you ask me, it's not even close. Marley May Applegate versus Wilhelmina Eugenia Shisbey. *No way, Jose.* Sorry, Mar, I win this, hands down.

"I'm going to the beach!" I yelled out to my dad, hearing the chop chop of his kitchen knife hitting the butcher block as he sliced carrots. My dad's sort of a nerd like me, and he has a garden in the backyard. Most California kids get a pool. I get an organic vegetable garden and smelly compost pile.

"Don't forget your sunscreen! And have fun!"

I let the front-door screen slam behind me and joined Marley seated on my front steps, her eyes closed and her face turned up to catch the sun. She was dressed in orange shorts, a geometric patterned T-shirt, and green flip-flops with plastic daisies glued on. Collectively, her outfit represented every color of the sherbets in the front counter at Baskin Robbins ice cream.

Because she's small for twelve, (Marley skipped a grade) her wardrobe choices are limited to the kids' section, which means Marley has a closet full of pastels and patterns and the occasional cartoon graphic tee—a look only she can pull off. Marley also wears pigtails she calls dreadlocks, but I say are curls she just doesn't brush.

As far as I'm concerned, in all of nerdom at

Triton Middle School, Marley reigns supreme. She could not care less what people think about her wardrobe choices. Unlike me, who can obsess over minutia, (darn OCD!) and is the reason I stick to a uniform that consists of a white long-sleeved button-down shirt, denim jeans, and black-and-white Converse sneakers whatever the season.

"Hey, Marley." I sat down beside her and gave her a little nudge. "Working on your tan?" I joked.

Marley's skin is the color of the outside of a Kit Kat bar, so it's not as if she needs to tan. Lucky duck. Not me, my skin is the same color as the inside of a Peppermint Pattie, white as snow. I burn to a crisp no matter how much sunscreen I glob on. Even this early into the game, I don't think sunny California is going to be a good match for me.

Marley nudged me back. "Hey yourself, four-eyes. Ready to go?" Marley didn't wait for me to answer and she stood up, dusting off her backside. She took her arm in mine and we started walking down the street toward the beach a few blocks away.

Marley's four-eyes remark is an inside joke.

There's not an unkind bone in Marley's body. Yes, I wear glasses—thick black-framed ones to help with my astigmatism and to keep my weak eye from ever turning back in. But that's not why Marley said it. The reason Marley calls me four-eyes is she insists I have eyes in the back of my head. Some sort of sixth sense, she tells me.

In a way, Marley's right. For some reason I can feel what people are feeling. Even if they are yards away from me, I can *feel* them. Their joy or their sorrow, or if they're angry or anxious. It's called empathy and it's probably from my years in the orphanage. And I don't want to get all Lemony Snicket on you about my days in the orphanage, because they weren't all terrible—if you don't count having to take baths with other kids or sleeping three to a bed, but it was hard not to suck up what the other kids were feeling. The sadness and the despair. The desperate desire to become part of a family.

Marley and I didn't make it four houses down the block before I gently untangled my arm from hers. As the new kid in town, I didn't want any of the other kids on our block to get the wrong idea about me. Or Marley. Not that there would be anything wrong if Marley liked girls in *that* way. To each his or her own, as far as I'm concerned. But Marley definitely wasn't gay or anything. She was affectionate to everyone—boys and girls—and so sometimes kids got the wrong idea about her.

Marley has suffered through more than her share of vicious rumors. Not only because of being named after a major Rasta stoner, but also because of the biracial thing, and the fact she's the editor of the school paper. Just last week, some brain-dead goofball wrote in red lipstick on Marley's locker, *Militant Marley for Congress.*

As if anyone who dresses like Rainbow Brite could be a radical. I'm so sure.

"Don't frown, Willa. It will give you wrinkles." Marley smiled at me. "You think too much. You need to learn to be more in the moment," she said, sounding like some New Age guru. Marley palmed the button on the light pole and we waited for it to say *walk.*

"*Omm* …" I chanted, closing my eyes and touching my thumbs to my index fingers in what I imagined was a close representation of the standard yoga finger position.

The light changed, and we crossed the busy intersection and turned right at the sidewalk heading towards the lifeguard station to meet up with members of our school's surf club for beach clean-up day. It was purely voluntary, but unlike Marley, who believes "it's our civic duty to protect Mother Earth who sustains us," I was only in it for the extra credit in my fourth period class.

Despite the closeness of the water and not yet 10:00 in the morning, I was starting to sweat. Maybe I needed to go to a tanning salon and build up a fake tan first, so I could wear a short-sleeved shirt like a normal person. Although most normal people don't have as much disgusting dark hair on their white arms as I have. Maybe a tan would at least lessen the contrast. I'd still have hairy arms, but on darker skin, (and the melanoma won't show up for another ten years, if I'm lucky).

My hair was making my neck sweat, so I pulled two rubber bands from my wrists and put my hair into pigtails before unbuttoning my shirt one button.

One button or five, it wouldn't have mattered, there's not much to see.

"So, who do you think will show up?" I asked, but especially caring about one *who* in particular.

Marley's face split in a big grin. "The way you're blushing, I know who you hope will be there." Marley fished a pair of neon green sunglasses out of her pocket and put them on. She scanned the beach and then pointed. "There's your guy right there. He's under the Surfrider tent."

My guy, Marley called him. *In my dreams …*

Cody Cassidy, the coolest of the cool, stood under the blue pop-up tent along with a half dozen other people, both kids and adults. He was leaning over the portable table instructing some blonde-haired girl where to sign in. She smiled at him—how could she *not?*—and Cody handed her some gloves and a trash bag from the pile on top of the table.

The event was co-sponsored by Hurley, so Cody was completely Hurleyed out, and he wore black Hurley board shorts with green neon stitching and drawstring, a classic Hurley T-shirt in green with black block lettering, and a black Sig Zane trucker hat covering his dark blond hair. I couldn't be sure from the distance, but it looked like he was wearing black flip-flops. Hurley Phantoms, maybe.

Six months ago, I wouldn't have known the difference between Hurley and girly, but then six months ago I wasn't living in Huntington Beach, just blocks away from the hottest boy I'd ever seen. And if I know anything at all about boys, (which I don't, so I had to break down and finally ask Olivia), it's that in order to interest a boy, you have to find some common ground. Olivia suggested I show an interest in whatever the boy liked. That's why I now have a current subscription to *Surfer Magazine*. I don't know shoot from shinola about girls' clothes, but I'm becoming a walking Wikipedia of the current trends in boy's surfing apparel.

I met Cody the first day at Triton. Not at the Friendship Bench, of course. Kids like him don't have to go looking for friends. Popular kids like Cody are the sun, the center of the solar system, and everyone else just revolves around them.

I met Cody in second period, at exactly 9:28 a.m., right after Mr. Spitzer finished taking roll. Mr. Spitzer mortified me beyond belief when he called the "newbie" up to the front of the room. He actually called me that—the *newbie*. As in, "Let's all meet the newbie, Wilhelmina Shisbey," which of course brought on coughs and giggles, because, come on, who else but me can lay claim to an old-fashioned name like Wilhelmina? Certainly no one in Orange County, California, where all the kids have these made-up sounding names their parents got from watching those Disney Channel teen shows.

Here's just a small sampling of the names: There are the twins, Dakota and Dallas, and their brother, Denver, who is Olivia's new boyfriend. According to Olivia, the Duncan kids are named after the places where they were conceived. But, hello!— there's a *North* and a *South* Dakota, and it's over a thousand miles from Rapid City, South Dakota, to Dallas, Texas. I may not know much about s-e-x, but I'm willing to bet my allowance you can't conceive twins in two different places that are a thousand miles apart.

Some of the other random names of my new California classmates are: Braden, Brylee, Hallie, Keiran, Griffen, Kirby, and Jax. Not Jack, but *Jax*.

J-A-X. And not to change the subject, but how is it possible almost all the kids at Triton Middle School have hair that is white-blonde, blonde-blonde, golden blonde, or blond*ish*? I mean, is it even statistically possible? Isn't it even *less* probable than two blue-eyed parents having a brown-eyed kid? You know, that broken gene, dominant trait thing?

Anyway … back to the story of how I met Cody.

I didn't immediately leap from my seat that day when Mr. Spitzer called me up, so he turned up the wick and he did this theatrical sweeping motion with his hands, and he bowed at the waist, inviting me up. On my way to the board, one of the Duncan twins intentionally pushed her backpack to the floor and I stumbled over it. Everybody laughed again— at the nerdy new kid tripping her way up the aisle. Cody, nice guy that he is, reached out a hand to steady me, which made it worse.

I couldn't tell if it was the girl with the city name or the one with the abbreviated state, but one of them said, "Eww, Cody," as if we were still in third grade and she thought maybe I had cooties or something.

Once I got to the front, I stuttered through my introduction, my heart hammering in my chest, before I finally managed to say, "My name is Wilhelmina, but people call me Willa."

"She looks more like Ugly Betty than Wilhelmina Slater," someone muttered, commenting on the *Ugly Betty* TV show, and not the first time I'd heard the line before.

"Yeah, right?" someone else said.

"True dat!" And it may have been the single black kid, Trey, in Wonder-Bread-white-land who said it, but I don't want to profile.

I took a deep breath and continued, looking out into the sea of faces and trying to picture the kids in their underwear like my dad once suggested in order to make public speaking easier, but it seemed wrong on *sooo* many levels, so I quit trying, and instead I stared down at the tops of my shoes. "I just moved here with my family from Lincoln Park. That's in Illinois, about four miles from the city of Chicago."

From the back of the room, a voice called out in falsetto, "I like to take long walks on the beach at sunset and my fondest dream is to someday marry

Nick Jonas."

Mr. Spitzer stopped shuffling the papers on his desk and glared at someone in the last row. "That's enough, Dylan."

Dylan slunk down in his seat, but gave a down-low high-five to the kid seated across the row from him.

"Thank you, Willa, you may sit down." Mr. Spitzer adjusted his gold wire-rimmed glasses and said the line I guess he's paid to say: "On behalf of the faculty, I'd like to formally welcome you to Triton Middle School. Class, let's all use some of our Dolphin spirit and welcome Willa."

A few kids said hi or hey and smiled, but most stayed silent, and a few stared me down, or maybe they sized me *up*. Whatever it was, it seemed slightly threatening.

One voice, however, rang out loud and clear. It was Cody's. "Welcome to sunny California, Chicago," he said, a genuine smile on his handsome face, and renaming me after the windy city. "You're gonna love it here."

CHAPTER 2

Cody raised his head from the sign-in table and he waved as we trudged in the sand over to the tent to pick up our gloves and trash bags. Well, I trudged—my sneakers quickly filling with sand with every step—and Marley skipped. Marley *skipped*. In flip-flops. In. The. Sand.

Marley's sort of a skipper. Maybe it's because she's so small and elfin-like. Elves seem like they'd be big skippers to me. But because Marley's my new BFF (and my only friend—period) I don't have the heart to tell her kids who are Mensa smart probably shouldn't skip.

"Hi, Cody," Marley chirped, her chin growing more pointed with her perkiness. "Where do I sign in?"

Cody held up his finger indicating he needed a second. "Thanks for your support, Ace! You rock, dude!" he yelled out over Marley's head to the wet-suited surfer who had signed in just before us. The surfer turned around and gave Cody the hang loose gesture, also known as the shaka sign, rotating his thumb and pinkie finger while holding his three middle fingers turned inward. Cody returned the gesture and the surfer tipped his head in acknowledgment before heading south on the beach, his wetsuit still sparkling with water, gloves and trash bag in hand.

Cody cut his light-brown eyes back to us and he smiled, his cheeks dimpling. Unlike Marley, who seemed unaffected by his nearness, my stomach did pole vaults.

"Hi, Marley. Hey, Willa. Thanks for coming."

"It's our civic duty," I lied, and earning me a look from Marley. I leaned towards the table to sign the liability release form and Marley did the same.

"On behalf of Hurley, the Surfrider Foundation, and the Surf Club of Triton Middle School, I'd like to thank you for your participation in this worthwhile cause," Cody said, reading the words off of the palm of his left hand, his voice sounding official. He lifted his eyes to us and his lips tugged in a lopsided smile.

I noticed his nose was burnt from the sun and even from across the table I could smell his sunscreen. It smelled like coconut.

"This might be easier." A tall guy with a shaved head and wearing a Surfrider T-shirt handed Cody an index card.

Cody took the card and then cleared his throat, (but in a jokey way) before saying, "This event is for four hours. Bottled water is available under the tent at no charge, as is sunscreen. For your protection we have provided plastic gloves and hand sanitizer. Please see that gloves, water bottles, and trash bags are disposed of in their proper receptacles. Etcetera, etcetera." He tossed the card on the table.

Marley pulled on one of the plastic gloves—one size fits *none*, from the box on the table. Because Marley's hands are so small, the glove folded in half. All three of us busted out laughing at the same time.

"Wait." Cody reached underneath the table. "Here ya go. We also have kids' sizes," he teased. He handed Marley a pair of gloves from a box marked "Women's Small."

I stuck with the standard issue size and pulled two from the box, trying them on for size. "Good enough, I guess." The tips of the gloves were unfilled, but it's not as though I was performing surgery or something. I wiggled my fingers at Marley.

Cody placed his palms on the table and leaned forward to look me over from feet to neck. He stepped back and crossed his arms across his chest, his forehead puckering into a frown underneath the brim of his hat. "Chicago, are you wearing something underneath all those clothes?"

Even though I knew what Cody was getting at, my cheeks burned with embarrassment at his words. In my defense, it was almost the third week in September—the twenty-first—for Pete's sake. One day short of fall. How was I supposed to know a September in California could be as hot as a July in Chicago?

"And darkness fell upon the face of the earth," Marley whispered from behind me.

As rotten luck would have it—in the middle of my just-kill-me-now moment, the terrible teens, Dakota and Dallas Duncan, reached the tent.

"Omigod, Cody! What a thing to ask Willa."

I haven't a clue which one said it. If it weren't for the fact one wore a pink sundress with spaghetti straps and one wore a purple one, they were identical, with their perfect figures and flawless flat-ironed hair cascading over their shoulders, not to mention big cornflower blue eyes (that were probably colored contacts).

My guess is Dakota said it. And I must have guessed correctly, because she leaned across the table to give Cody some phony air kiss thing where she put her head to the side of each of his cheeks without ever touching his face, and she made some "mmwaw, mmwaw" sound. So, yeah, it must have been Dakota, his girlfriend.

"What Cody wants to know, *I'm sure*," Dakota said to me before looking at Cody for confirmation. Cody nodded, figuring out where she was headed. "Where is your proper beach *attire*?" She accentuated the word, sounding all hoity toity. "Surely you own shorts or a bathing suit. Haven't you ever been to a beach before? I know they have an ocean and beaches in Chicago," Miss Know It All explained. "I've seen the pictures."

"And what ocean would that be, Dakota?" Marley asked sweetly, setting Dakota up for the fall.

Cody took off his hat, ruffled his hair, and then placed the hat back on his head with the brim facing the back. Shaking his head, he said, "Dakota, that wasn't an ocean. It was Lake Michigan, the third largest of the five Great Lakes of North America."

Dakota and Dallas' jaws dropped, as if it was inconceivable Cody would know simple geography, and their pastel painted lips formed an O, reminding me of the koi I'd seen at the Chicago Botanic Garden at feeding time.

"If it's Lake Michigan, what's it doing in Illinois? Wouldn't Lake Michigan be *in* Michigan?" Dakota said, flustered. Her sister nodded her head but stayed silent. Dakota made a face and waved her hands dismissively, her bangle bracelets jangling. "*Whatever!*"

Dallas broke her silence. "Aren't you hot, Willa? It's summer at the beach and you're wearing winter clothes. Isn't your dad a dentist? Can't dentists afford to buy their children clothes? Or is this outfit some kind of school uniform where you're from?" She waved her bubblegum-pink manicured finger at me. "In which case—newsflash, Chicago girl—it's Saturday, and you're allowed to wear whatever you want."

If I was hot before, I was now ten degrees hotter under their attack.

"I got it!" Dakota squealed, just as another group of kids from our class made their way to the sign-in table. Erik, Brylee, Hallie, and Jax crowded under the shade of the tent, and all wearing shorts and assorted tank tops, several of them barefoot. "I know why you wear long-sleeved shirts and long pants. You're a Cullen! That's it. *You're a vampire.* You'd have to be the homely cousin or something, because all of the Cullens are gorgeous," she trailed off. "But it all makes sense now … the strange accent. The keen ability to recall certain events. The super-white skin that has to be covered up so we don't see your flesh *'sparkle like tiny diamonds …'*" She used her fingertips for dramatic effect while repeating the phrase from the *Twilight* book series when Bella sees Edward with his shirt off for the first time.

"Stop it, Dakota. That's enough. Leave her alone," Cody said.

Marley grabbed my hand and started to pull. I willed myself not to cry while Marley dragged me into the hot sun. "Come on, Willa, there's some trash with our name on it."

"You got that right," Dakota said smugly and folding her arms tightly across her chest.

"Dakota, quit!" Cody hissed at her.

Marley headed out toward the pier, stopping every few feet to pick up cigarette butts or empty bottles, tossing them in her trash bag.

I bent down to use my gloved hand to pick up a broken flip-flop and a crushed Pepsi can, blinking away my tears. "Do they know about me, Marley?" I gingerly grabbed a wet plastic baggie containing a moldy sandwich to add to my trash bag.

Marley sat in the sand and started collecting the cigarette butts that littered a four-foot diameter around her. She reached and dropped, reached and dropped, grimacing as she picked up every soggy butt.

"Know *what*, Willa? That you're really a vampire?" Marley smiled at me, trying to lighten my mood.

I plopped down in the sand beside her and took off my left shoe. I emptied it slowly, watching the grains of sand pour from it and forming a small mound.

"I *wish*." Then I wouldn't have to live in sunny California. I could be in Canada. Or Michigan for that matter; it's cold enough. I emptied the sand in my other shoe. "Do the kids know I have H-SAM, Marley? Is that what Dakota meant about my 'keen ability to recall certain events?' Have you told someone?"

Marley was the only person in California outside my family and the doctors at UCI who knew my secret. Or at least the only person who *I* told. And I doubt my dad or Diane said anything. Diane tried to blab to the news once, back in Chicago, and my dad went ballistic.

"Your secrets are safe with me, Willa." Marley paused from her butt duty and drew a picture in the sand with a piece of driftwood. It was of flowers and trees, and surprisingly accurate for using a stick. "But isn't your sister sort of dating the brother of the Megamind twins? Maybe she said something to him and he told his sisters."

"Oh, jeez!" I collapsed back in the sand and covered my face with my forearm.

Olivia. Of course! When she told Blaine I was an autistic savant, I assumed she was just dramatizing for effect. But she promised! Olivia promised me she wouldn't say anything. I'm already an outsider. How will I ever fit in if people know I'm a freak?

"Maybe the kids will think you have some cool superpower," Marley said, trying to make me feel better with her unrealistic optimism.

I removed my arm and turned on my side, playing with the warm sand. "Yeah, sure. Because that's exactly how this works. Odd and weird are synonymous with superheroes."

Marley quit her drawing and tipped her head to the side. "Actually, Willa, they are. Think about it. Every single superhero was born of tragedy and most were orphans, like you." Marley took off her sunglasses, tucking them on the front of her shirt, and she put on her *must I explain everything* expression. "Captain America was a kid who survived polio and later became a super-soldier, modeling courage and hope in the face of insurmountable foes. Billy Batson was an orphan who fought against prejudice and discrimination, later becoming Captain Marvel, protector of the universe. That story has a lot of sci-fi and is waaay too complicated for me to easily explain—but you get the picture."

"I guess," I said, but not really meaning it.

Marley was on a mission to make a point. "And *all* of the X-Men—the first major ones, anyway—were mutants born with genetic anomalies that gave them great abilities. They were actually the first superheroes to set the stage to right human indignities."

I still wasn't impressed. I collect erasers, not comic books.

"There's Superman. You may have heard of *him*. Biggest superhero of all time?" Marley raised her eyebrows and threw a cigarette butt at me. It hit me on the leg and bounced off my jeans. I picked it up and put it in my bag. Marley continued, "Clark Kent was—here it comes, are you ready?—yet another orphan. He used the earth's environment to activate his incredible powers in order to save the world."

Marley started to tick superhero names off her fingers. "Batman? Orphan. A guy who was just your average Joe without any special powers but with more money than Jehovah, who dedicated his life to prevent and avenge crimes. Spiderman? Total orphan. Although he had that really great aunt and uncle who raised him. There was a kid who struggled with social interaction and suffered from bullying. After he got bitten by the spider, he changed, and he began to use his power to protect those who couldn't protect themselves."

It took a minute to sink it, but I actually got what Marley was trying to say. And yeah, so maybe it was just the tiniest bit lame—Marley's superhero analogies—but her point was taken.

I stood up and brushed the sand from my legs. "Marley, you're the best!" I reached out a hand to help her up and then hugged her tightly to me.

"Lesbos!" someone yelled from the top of the pier. It was too far away to see who, and honestly? I didn't care.

I stepped away from Marley and bent down to pick up our trash bags. I handed Marley hers and we started walking slowly up the beach, bending down every few minutes to add more trash to the rapidly filling bags.

A thought occurred to me. "Dakota's the spider. Right, Marley? In your last analogy, Dakota is the spider from *Spiderman* and I'm supposed to become the Peter Parker. I'll eventually get stronger because of her venom."

Marley sighed and her shoulders slumped slightly. She put her sunglasses back on just as a gentle wind sprang up and fluffed her kinky curls. Her expression turned thoughtful. Marley is what people would call an "old soul."

"The spider is the amalgamation of people like Dakota and Dallas—and your sister too, from what you tell me. I haven't known you for long, Willa, but I believe you could possibly become the Peter Parker of our school. Wilhelmina Shisbey—*Spider-girl.*"

"Spider-girl," I repeated, and even though I'm a total arachnophobe, I liked the sound of it.

Marley bent to pick up another piece of trash. She threw it out toward the ocean when it proved to be a barnacled seashell. "Willa, I don't want to hurt your feelings, but may I offer you one tiny piece of advice?" Marley blushed slightly under her naturally dark coloring.

"Sure. Fire away." I tried to tighten my gloves around my wrists, with little success.

"If you don't want people to know about your superior memory, maybe tone down the dates, weather channel, what-I-had-for-breakfast thing you do."

"*What?* What date and what weather channel thing?" And okay, so maybe once or twice I told Marley what I had for breakfast in the past, but that's because breakfast is my favorite meal. I adore Frosted Flakes. They're g-r-r-r-reat!

"You know. That thing you do."

"No, Marley, I *don't* know," I said, sounding harsher than I intended.

"Don't get mad, Willa. I'm only trying to help."

"Then tell me. What *exactly* is it I do?"

"Promise you won't hate me?"

"No, Marley. I won't hate you." Although by then I was getting majorly annoyed with her.

"Positive?" she asked.

"Positive."

Marley did her best to imitate me, and her attempt wasn't half-bad. "Your brother was born on January sixteenth, you say? Then it was a Sunday and in Chicago the temperature was sixty-nine degrees with an altostratus cloud covering and a strong wind coming from the north. I had Golden Grahams for breakfast."

"For your information, *Marley Applegate*, it was a Friday, the coldest day on record for the entire year, and the temperature was a *minus* seventeen degrees. Plus, there wasn't any wind."

As far as the cloud cover, I never can remember the differences between cirrus, stratus, and cumulus, so there was a slight chance Marley was right about the clouds—just like she was right about my need to report the daily weather from my past. *And* about sharing the details of the most important meal of the day.

Oh, brother, I am a total loser.

I headed farther down the beach, away from Marley.

"See? You're mad!" Marley shouted out to me.

"No! I'll be fine. Just give me a few minutes. I'll work closer to the water and meet you in five!" I shouted back. Marley waved and I headed north toward the pier.

CHAPTER 3

Marley was right. How lame—my dates, and the weather thing, and my obsession with boxed cereal. But I can't help it. At least I don't *think* I can help it. Not that I wouldn't give it my best effort to try, now that Marley pointed out how annoying it was.

The thing with H-SAM is one single memory can open the floodgates and bring on an entire string of them. For some H-SAMers, their memory works like the scene selection menu on a DVD. Little movies in a continuum.

For me, dates seem to be a big trigger, and I see the memories almost as if they are on pages of a calendar. The memory of one day comes back and then leads to the next day and the next, peeling off the calendar, the same way they do it in old movies to show the passing of time. Plus, every memory comes back in the same amount of detail as the day it happened. The temperature of the day, the color of the sky, what I was watching on TV, what I was wearing, or what crappy thing Olivia did to me, or the hurtful things Diane said.

And all of them—the memories—come back just as vividly, and with the same amount of emotion as when they first happened, the same as in real time. So I have to relive all the bad stuff a million times over.

Honestly? H-SAM totally sucks.

I spent a few minutes picking up three rusted cans, two dog-eaten Frisbees—one red and one yellow—and a Del Taco bag shredded by the seagulls. Next, I wandered closer to the water and reached down to pick up a plastic baggie filled with water and soggy Goldfish—the small fish-shaped crackers, not the actual fish—chuckling at the irony of it.

The Surfrider pamphlet said to be especially conscious of plastic or rubber because they don't break down like glass and metal. Not only do they pollute the ocean, but they also kill the birds and the fish when they choke on it and die.

I tossed the baggie into my trash bag and hefted it on my shoulder, trudging closer to the water's edge to find more litter.

The heat was relentless despite the closeness of the water. Sweat slowly began to trickle down my face, fogging my glasses. As much as I hated admitting Her Evilnesses were right, I was starting to wish I'd gone with a better choice of beachwear.

Not a dress or short shorts like the rest of the girls, but, rather, something my dad calls Bermuda shorts and I call a pant that can't make up its mind. Too long to be considered shorts and too short to be capris, Bermuda shorts are the half-breeds of the apparel world. Shunned by the majority of the world's population, Bermudas have found a safe haven in certain coastal retirement communities, and to a lesser extent, in the bottom dresser drawer of one Willa Eugenia Shisbey.

I took off my glasses and wiped the sweat from my forehead with the back of my hand. Even with my glasses off, I could see a few water-filled baggies in the wet sand less than a foot from me. "Pigs," I muttered, reaching down to get the one nearest to me.

"Ahhh!" I screamed, as searing hot pain shot through my right hand. I dropped the bag back in the water and fumbled to put my glasses back on. It wasn't plastic. *It was a jellyfish!* "November 25th, 2016!" I yelled. And then louder, "November 25th, 2016!" repeating myself like an actual autistic savant and their habit of repeating things.

Friday, November 25th, 2016 was the day I read an article on the Internet site Our Deadly Planet about how an animal 95 percent water and has no brain, (and actually eats and poops out of the same opening) is one of the deadliest creatures on Earth.

My entire body, except for my hand—which pulsed in indescribable pain with every beat of my heart—started to feel numb as the venom spread through my body. *"Dead in minutes…"* I moaned, while my vision started to blur, and I tried to recall the specific details of the article I had only skimmed, more interested in the colorful pictures. "Help!" I gasped clutching my hands to my throat and trying to breathe. "Help!" I tore at the top buttons of my shirt desperate for air.

Think. Think. Was it humans or sea turtles the toxic venom killed in minutes? I tried racking my poisoned brain to remember what the article said and wishing H-SAM actually had purpose, like a photographic memory.

Or maybe the article said it was prawns that died quickly, and for humans it was a slow and agonizing death. Was it prawns? My breath was now shallow and I'd lost all feeling in my feet. I dropped to my knees and started crawling up the shore, grasping at the sand to propel me forward, knowing it would only be a matter of time before I lost consciousness.

Snippets of the article popped in and out of my mind. *Out of the five most poisonous jellyfish on the planet, the box jellyfish is the most deadly creature on Earth. Unlike the Portuguese Man o' War, the box jellyfish kills…* The memory of the article ended there because Diane arrived home from the grocery store and yelled she bought me a new supply of sweetened cereal, and of course, I couldn't resist. Darn the allure of Fruity Pebbles!

With numb hands, I scratched my way up the

last few feet of sand. Using the last ounce of my strength, I turned over so I could die facing the sun.

"Friends applaud, the comedy is over," I choked out uttering Beethoven's—and my—last words.

***

Either Marley was my guide into the bright light of the everlasting or it wasn't my time to go, because I woke up to see Marley's concerned face looking down at me.

"How are you feeling?" Marley offered her hand to help me sit up and then she handed me a bottle of water.

I looked around and saw I was lying on a cot underneath a pop-up tent that served as a first aid station for the event. Around me lifeguards were assisting several other people and applying sunscreen and ointment to the sunburned and injured, although, unlike me, they were all seated in chairs, not sprawled on a ratty cot while their equally ratty and beginning-letter-of-the-alphabet-sized bra showed because the buttons of their shirt were now missing. I tugged my shirt together with my left hand and took the offered bottle of water with my right, surprised that except for some slight redness, it didn't look like there was much damage.

"What happened?" I asked, taking a sip of the cold water. Marley noticed my shirt dilemma, and she removed a safety pin from the bottom of her shirt, handing it to me.

"You got stung by a jellyfish and then you hyperventilated and fainted. Cody found you and alerted the lifeguard, and then he carried you here. The lifeguard. Not Cody. Not that Cody couldn't have carried you," she finished, giving me a dimpled smile, "because I'm sure he could have."

Saying his name must have had the power to summon him, and the tent suddenly brightened with his presence when he entered and gave me a lopsided grin while heading over our way. Unfortunately, it darkened just as quickly when in walked Dakota, Dallas, Griffen, Brylee, and Jax, all of them coming over to cluster around me.

Cody shifted in the sand and looked embarrassed. "Uhh ... sorry, Chicago. I guess I should have warned you to be on the lookout for jellyfish masquerading as plastic bags. But I appreciate your passion for the cause. Are you feeling any better? I know it can hurt like a son of a gun when those suckers sting you, but the pain is usually gone within an hour. Lucky for you, it was a purple-striped jelly and they aren't poisonous."

Dakota suddenly grabbed her neck with both of her hands and started shrieking, "Help me! Help me! I'm dying," before dramatically falling to the sand in what I assumed was a reenactment of the event, but looked as if she were trying to sizzle like bacon. Dallas, thinking it was flippin' hilarious, quickly followed suit, followed by Jax, who not only undulated uncontrollably, but also used his spit to make it seem as if he were foaming at the mouth.

"Stop it!" Marley told them, springing up from her chair and stomping her foot in the sand.

"Come on, guys, let it go," Cody said. "Dakota, quit it!" He held out his hand to help her up, but she ignored him and she sizzled some more.

A muscled lifeguard with long blond hair finished applying a cartoon bandage to a toddler's scraped knee and then headed our way. "Okay, guys, the fun is over. Back to trash duty."

Dakota and Dallas got up from the sand, brushing their legs while Jax left it to coat him in a layer of crust like a breaded chicken tender. Their fun cut short, the group gathered their trash bags and started shuffling their way from the tent, still laughing.

"Can you believe she actually thought she was dying?" Dakota said loud enough for me and everyone else under the tent to hear. "How lame."

"Well, it can really hurt when you get stung." I think it was Brylee who said it, but I was hiding my face in my hands, so I couldn't swear on it.

"My dad says pee is the best way to treat a jellyfish sting," Jax offered.

"Eww!" The girls all said in unison, their laughter fading as they headed down shore.

I felt Cody's hand touch my shoulder. "Don't let them get to you, Chicago," he said.

My eyes stung and I prayed for a tsunami. One big giant wave to come and sweep me out to the sea and away from all of this. The embarrassment. The contempt. The heat. And worst of all, Cody's pity.

"I'm not a moron!" I shouted out to them, not that they could have heard me. And then I tried to explain to Cody. "It's just that … I thought … I mean …" My stuttering wasn't helping matters. I cleared my throat and tried again, "I read on the Internet …"

Cody laughed. "Yeah, that Internet stuff will get you every time. I was once convinced I had cancer because my hiccups wouldn't go away. Turns out, I didn't have esophageal cancer, it was my addiction to Pop Rocks that caused them."

I appreciated what Cody was trying to do, not that it made me feel any better, and not that I necessarily believed him.

"You're cleared for release," the lifeguard said, coming over and handing me a piece of paper documenting my humiliation. "We tried to call your parents, but it went to voicemail. Do you want us to try again?"

I shook my head and gathered up my things. "I don't live far. I can walk." But what I really wanted to do was to run. Run away from this new place where I didn't fit in and run back to my old town and my old school, where, I didn't necessarily fit in, but at least was invisible enough not to be a laughingstock. I bolted from the tent without saying good-bye to Marley or thanking Cody for alerting the lifeguard and then sticking up for me. I know I should have, but I just couldn't.

Marley soon caught up with me. She's little, but she's fast.

"*Spider-girl, Spider-girl*," Marley encouraged, slightly out of breath and using her coach-on-the-field voice. "Don't let them get to you, Willa. They're like a toddler having a tantrum. Ignore them and they'll stop just as soon as they realize no one is watching." Marley hooked her slender arm through mine. "Come on. I'll walk you home."

"Chicago! Hey. Hold up." Cody jogged up to us and fell in step beside me. The sand went soft, and he accidentally touched his shoulder to mine. "Can I talk to you for a second?"

Marley winked at me and said, "On second thought," as she unhooked her arm from mine. "You look like you're feeling better, so maybe I'll stay behind and help a little longer." She gave me a little wave and headed out toward the water.

Cody pulled off his shirt while we walked, clueless about the effect it had on me with his surfer-toned torso and skin bronzed by the sun. I stumbled in the sand but quickly righted myself.

"Don't mind Dakota. She's not always so mean.

I think she must be PMSing."

"I didn't know Death Eaters suffered from PMS."

Cody burst out laughing, but immediately sobered when he saw I wasn't smiling. He quickly changed the subject. "Tell me something, Chicago. How's math going for you?" he asked conversationally.

Cody sits behind me in math class. Math is the bane of my existence. It's Algebra1 and not AP, the class Marley took.

"Better for me than for you, apparently. I saw your last test paper. C minus, wasn't it? Did your pencil run out of lead? It looked like half of your answers were missing." (Unlike my paper—a plain C—where half of my answers were simply incorrect.)

"No, my pencil was fine. But it's a long story. I'll tell it to you sometime over a cold one."

"A cold one?" I wasn't sure I heard Cody right.

"Kidding! Chicago, dude, you've got to learn to lighten up."

Lighten up? Sure, it was easy for Cody to say. He wasn't the one who practically had to have CPR because of an anxiety attack and now was the joke of the eighth grade. This was Cody, the rich kid, whose parents own three McDonald's restaurants and who lives in a McMansion on the water in Huntington Harbor. The outgoing guy who is boy-band beautiful, with hair naturally streaked blond by the sun, and who even looks good wearing hats. Cody, the kid who can surf better, skateboard faster, and snowboard longer than any other kid in school.

Cody. Everyone's favorite person, and the boyfriend of Dakota—the girl who seemed determined to make my life miserable.

We passed another Surfrider tent, and Cody grabbed two waters from the table. I'd never had so much water in one day in my life. Unscrewing the first one, he handed it to me. Next, he unscrewed his and then tipped his bottle to mine in a toast before gulping it down and spilling some on his bare chest. He used his shirt to wipe it.

I forced myself to pull my eyes away and look at his face.

"Why do you want to know how math is going for me? Specific point or general question?"

I sipped on my tenth bottle of water and noticed except for the tiniest red mark, my hand was fine.

Of course my psyche, my pride, and my reputation were now permanently damaged. But on the upside, I was thrilled beyond belief to be standing next to Cody, just the two of us, while forty feet away Dakota Duncan and her friends were otherwise occupied — gouging a dead pelican's eyeballs out of its sockets with a stick of driftwood.

Cody capped his water and pointed the bottle at me. "I thought I might be able to help you out. Believe it or not, I'm actually pretty good in math. In fact, I'm *really* good in math. But shhh ..." he dropped his voice to a whisper and put his finger to his lips. "Don't tell anybody. I don't want to blow my cover."

"Yeah, right. Sure you are. If I need a tutor, I can have Marley help me."

Immediately I realized what a moron I was. A total and complete moron! Cody was offering to tutor me. *Me!* The new girl. The lame-o from Chicago.

Cody did a lay-up and threw his water bottle in the trashcan next to the tent. "Score!" he yelled, before turning back to me. "Okay. Don't believe me. See if I care!" Cody pretended to toss his hair over his shoulder like a girl.

I didn't want to lose the opportunity Cody was presenting. To actually have the chance to hang out with Cody, alone. Or as alone as one can be in a family of four that included Olivia and Diane, two people who made it their mission to add to my life's misery, so I rushed out. "No! Yes! I mean … sure. Absolutely. Of course I could use your help. How soon do you want to start?"

Cody smiled at my discomfort. "How about after school on Monday? My place or yours?"

"My place," I said, praying Olivia had cheer practice and Diane was too busy gearing up for her audition for that OC housewife show to be home.

"Monday it is."

CHAPTER 4

Olivia barged into my room without knocking. She was dressed in a fuzzy white robe and pink slippers, and her hair was wet and covered in a towel. She stopped in her tracks when she caught me mid-pull, before I quickly tugged down the bottom of a tight blue V-neck, long sleeved T-shirt, tucking it into the top of my jeans.

"Is that my shirt?" she demanded. "Oh my god, you are so wearing my shirt! *Mommm!*" she yelled into the hallway. "Willa is wearing my favorite shirt," she tattled. Olivia needn't have bothered yelling. Diane had left for Pilates thirty minutes ago and Dad would only tell Olivia for the hundredth time she needed to learn to share.

"This is not your shirt. Don't you think I'd

remember if it was your shirt?" I calmly said, slipping my feet into my sneakers and then going to my dresser to get my glasses. I put them on and then brushed my hair, putting it into a low side ponytail and securing it with a thick black rubber band.

I was lying. The shirt did belong to Olivia, but that's one of the few perks of having H-SAM. Olivia knows I remember stuff and for the most part I don't usually lie. So if I tell Olivia it's not her shirt, she believes me. Just the same way she believes me when I tell her she needs to wear her yellow sweater and her black skinny jeans today because it's a Monday, and the last time she wore that same outfit it was a Thursday, three months ago. You could say, in a way, I'm sort of like Olivia's dresser. I tell her which of her outfits it's okay to wear so she doesn't ever wear the same thing more than twice in a semester.

Truth be known, it's all a lie. In fact, I just lied when I said a second ago I don't usually lie. When it comes to Olivia, I lie every day. And I'm so good at it too!

Olivia: "When did I last wear my flouncy patterned skirt with my denim vest?"

Me—lying: "It was a Wednesday, the second week in May, and you were going shopping after school with Melody. Wear the skirt, but pair it with your slouchy pink top instead."

Olivia: "Didn't I wear this blazer with my Diesel jeans just last week?"

Me—lying: "Last week? Try last *year*. I think you must have some memory problems."

Olivia: "Rachel says I wore this same dress now three times this month."

Me—lying: "Who you gonna believe, a girl who thinks the moon landing was nothing but a fraud, or your own sister?"

My main goal in life is to dress Olivia in the same clothes on the same day of every month of every year (until she grows out them). Including accessories. And twice a month if she's being especially mean to me. It's my own silent war. Because, here's a kink to H-SAM—it's *autobiographical.* Meaning—it's all about me. H-SAM is the affliction of the narcissist, one could say. I don't know and I don't care what Olivia wears. She could wear her bedspread for all I care. Or her drapes. They're a better color for her.

I went to the kitchen and quickly wolfed down a bowl of Cap'n Crunch. Delish. When I was through, I put my dishes in the dishwasher and went into my dad and Diane's bedroom to kiss my dad good-bye.

I know it's not cool to love your dad, but I do. I totally do. For one thing, he's super nice to me, and I know he means it when he says he's glad I'm his daughter. (Unlike Diane who is only nice to me if other people are around and who secretly hopes my birth mom will someday come claim me.) Plus, how can you *not* love a guy who looks at a homely glasses-wearing orphan kid with a cleft lip and two extra incisors that make her look like a snarling Chihuahua, and who thinks to himself, "Now there's a child I'd like to make part of my family!"

My dad and I even look genetically related, with the same shape and color to our brown eyes and our straight brown hair. People often comment on the resemblance, and when they do, you should see Diane's face! Honestly, her skin gets all red and blotchy and she looks as if she's about ready to stroke-out. Diane knows better than to correct them with the "Willa is adopted" bit if my dad is around. She did that once and my dad ripped her a new one.

The other reason we look alike is our matching glasses. It's bad enough when moms want to play twinsies with their daughters and wear matching outfits, but wearing the same glasses as your dad really pushes the envelope. I know my dad would let me change mine, but that Tuesday, November 4th (Election Day), at 12:39, when my dad took us to LensCrafters and said, "My *daughter* and I will both take a pair of those," was one of my all-time favorite memories.

Someday I'll change mine, or maybe even get LASIK, and a small part of me will mourn.

I stood by the bedroom door and watched as my dad pulled a brown sock on his left foot and then a black one on his right but let it go. It's not as if anyone would see his socks when he was elbow-deep inside their mouth.

"Dad, is it okay if Cody Cassidy tutors me today after school? He'd be coming here to the house."

"The boy you talk about with the two brothers and the parents who own those McDonald's franchises? Sure, pumpkin. But remember Mom's rule. You need to keep your bedroom door open."

First of all, the open-door rule Dad was referring to applied to Olivia, not to me. And it wasn't a rule she followed. Before today, boys in my room remained a statistical impossibility, so it was never addressed.

Second, my dad knows even after eight years of being a Shisbey, I don't consider Diane my mom, and I probably never will. And I know for a fact Diane will never think of me as her daughter. (If love is a two-way street, Diane and I are in speeding cars and travelling on opposite sides of the road.) But that doesn't prevent my Dad from constantly emphasizing the word "Mom," and hoping if he *Mom, Mom, Mom—Mom's* me to death, I'll get it in my thick head Diane is my mother.

I wouldn't say Diane hates me, exactly, but I know she regrets that my dad ever met me.

I remember the first day I met my dad, when he introduced himself as Dr. Shisbey and brought me inside the director's office, seating me on one of those molded plastic chairs where it sounds like a heinie hiccup every time your bare thigh moves against the seat.

Once I settled in the chair, he gave me a big smile with the whitest teeth I've ever seen. They were practically blinding, they were so white, and they matched his lab coat. Reaching into his coat pocket, he pulled from it a tiny pepperoni pizza about the size of a dime. He told me it was a collectable eraser and not to eat it. Even as little as I was, I figured if a doctor was giving me a present, he was buttering me up for something.

Sure enough, he was, because then he handed me a small mirror and told me to look at my reflection. Preschooler or not, I knew there was a definite problem. Not only could I see it, the cleft that looked like a huge cut running from my upper lip to my nose, but I felt it; the split that made it hard for me to drink from a cup without the help of a straw and gave me a lisp the other kids made fun of.

As if that wasn't bad enough, I also had the lazy eye thing going on back then. Not always, but from time to time. Honestly, when I think about it now, no wonder my birth mother unloaded me. What a wreck!

Dr. Shisbey explained he was going to pull two of my teeth because I had too many of them. (Those extra pointed incisors.) And a different doctor—a plastic surgeon—would fix the cut on my upper lip—my cleft, he called it, before saying, "So you don't have to keep hanging around this place."

Even as young as I was, and even though he made it sound jokey, I got what he meant.

He meant he and his team were going to fix me, and then maybe I'd have a chance at adoption. Not that he or anyone at the home ever said, *"Fix the ugly kid so someone takes her."* But I'd hear the staff whisper things about me from time to time, not knowing exactly what they meant when they said words like "hard to place" or "physical deformity."

After the surgery I definitely looked better, but I wasn't going to win any awards either, and after years of finding me still at Children's Home each time he came to work on our teeth, my dad figured he'd better adopt me—and quick. He knew the game. (And no, in case you're wondering, an orphanage is NOT like a dog pound, in that they don't put you to sleep if no one wants you.)

What my dad knew is it wouldn't be long before they transferred me to foster care on account of my age. Don't let anyone tell you otherwise, foster care is no picnic. It's one home after another until you're eighteen, and then you're literally kicked to the curb and left to fend for yourself.

I know it wasn't a *total* pity adoption, because I could tell my dad always had a soft spot for me. He said I was quirky, but plucky. I didn't exactly know what either of those words meant and I thought plucky meant "without feathers" and that Dr. Shisbey thought I resembled the dead chickens the cook hacked into pieces on Mondays when we had fried chicken for dinner. He also said we were "two peas in a pod," because people considered him quirky too.

With all the euphemisms and unfamiliar words I didn't understand most of what he said, but he smiled and stroked my hair when he said it, so I assumed it was something nice.

Diane was against the adoption from the beginning—as Olivia continues to remind me on a weekly basis.

The first time I heard my dad and Diane argue about me, (I had gotten up to go pee and I heard my name, so I stood on the other side of the door to listen) it was a Wednesday night, six months after I came to live with them. They were in their bedroom and Dad sounded mad, asking Diane why she never kissed me goodnight, like she did to Olivia.

"I just can't seem to warm up to her, Ted," I heard Diane say. "I want to, but I can't. She's just so …" It took a few seconds before Diane found the appropriate word. "Odd," Diane blurted as the tears filled my eyes and began to trickle down my cheeks. "That child is just so odd."

Then Diane admitted she would never have agreed to the adoption if my dad hadn't taken her to see the musical *Annie* for their wedding anniversary just weeks before he asked her to agree. Diane said she got swept up in the moment, thinking of all of those precious raggedy orphan kids washing dirty dishes while singing their little hearts out. (Her words.)

The night after I listened to them talk about me, I came up with a plan to get Diane to like me. I found a tattered flannel nightgown of Olivia's in the rag drawer in the garage and after dinner I shrugged it on over my clothes and came into the kitchen belting out my best rendition of "It's The Hard-Knock Life" while clearing the dirty dishes from the table.

Diane wasn't impressed. In fact, she seemed mad and told me to stop acting silly. I must have made an impression on my dad though, because he started crying. Not because he was sad, but because he was laughing so hard he just about fell off his chair.

So, you see? I don't consider Diane my mom, and certainly not my mother. Not now. Not ever. Dad is my dad, *and* he's my father, in a way I can't quite explain, but Diane will never be more than the woman who is married to my dad.

My dad pulled me to him for a quick hug and wished me a good day.

***

"No! *No, no, no!*" I gasped in disbelief when I

arrived at my locker. The blood drained from my face and my fingers starting to tingle in a way that made me know I'd stopped breathing and was on the verge of hyperventilating again. I dropped my backpack and stared in horror. *Just breathe ... just breathe ... just breathe ...*

Crowding around my locker, laughing and pointing, seemed to be half of Triton Middle School and the skeezy-looking janitor—a college dropout that everyone calls Bob even though his name is Walter.

And the reason they were all crowding around my locker was because it was covered, and I mean *covered* in water-filled plastic baggies and crudely drawn pictures of jellyfish and what looked to be a picture of me with my hands around my neck and the words "Help! I'm dying!"

One sign was misspelled and read "Wierdo," in red marker, with the i before the e. Another read "Loser" written in black crayon. They were all taped haphazardly to my locker with gray duct tape. A couple of the boys used their hands to mimic choking and another grabbed one of the baggies from my locker and then threw it to the ground, yelling, "It bit me! It bit me!"

The baggie broke open when it hit the floor and made a small puddle. The boy next to him, a seventh grader I think, snatched another water-filled baggie from my locker and threw it at the first. Water and chaos rained down as a full-scale water fight started and the girls all shrieked and tried to get out of the way so the water wouldn't ruin their clothes and makeup.

The air behind me shifted and I felt Cody before I heard him. "Not cool," he said, laying a hand on my shoulder to comfort me. Marley came up alongside me and stared, along with a couple of kids who ran the school paper with her.

The door to the front office down the hall opened just as the first bell rang and Ms. Merchant, the assistant principal, stomped over, elbowing her way through the crowd. "What on *earth* is going on?" she roared. "Who is responsible for this?"

The chances of the culprit jumping up to exclaim Me! were slim to none, so I don't know why she even bothered to ask. All eyes dropped to the floor, including Dakota's and Dallas's, but I saw them link their pinkies and smile.

"Go. Go!" Ms. Merchant demanded, waving off the kids. They started to shuffle in various directions, laughing and chuckling and making more stupid comments. "Clean this up!" she said to Bob. Bob nodded and went to grab a mop and a trashcan.

"Sorry, Willa." Marley sighed and gave my shoulder a squeeze. Here." She dug her hand inside her pocket. "Maybe this will help." She took a folded piece of paper from inside her skirt pocket and handed it to me, tucking my fingers around it.

I opened it. *Spider-girl*, it read, in Marley's beautiful cursive, and she'd drawn a detailed picture of a superhero girl who looked sorta like me. Underneath the picture there was a quote. "*Never forget that the most powerful force on earth is love.*" ~ Nelson Rockefeller.

A lone tear escaped. "Thank you, Marley," I whispered, and brushed away the tear with the back of my palm.

"To class, Mr. Cassidy," Ms. Merchant said. "And remove your hat. You know the dress code."

"Yes, ma'am." Cody pulled his hat off his head. Hat in hand, he casually draped his arm across the back of my shoulders while I tried not to faint at his closeness. "I'll see you in math class, Chicago. Hang tough," he encouraged, pulling me to him in a quick side hug. He removed his arm and strutted away, pulling his black knit cap back on as soon as he rounded the corner.

Marley struggled over her good-bye to me, her expression soft and her eyes glittery with emotion. She gave my hand another quick squeeze before joining the newspaper kids and heading down the hall.

"Come with me, Wilhelmina. I'll give you an excused-tardy slip." Ms. Merchant headed for the office, her heels clip-clopping down the hallway.

Having little choice, I reached down and picked up my backpack and followed Ms. Merchant.

CHAPTER 5

Cody Cassidy was in my bedroom.
Cody Cassidy was in my bedroom!

And he was sitting on my bed! On top of sheets I may never wash again.

"Is this considered paisley?" Cody traced the blue-and-white swirly pattern of my comforter with his finger.

I sat at my desk and stared at him from across the room trying to work some spit back into my mouth so I could speak. "Uh-huh," was all I could manage.

Cody lifted his head and eyed the calendars that lined my walls with military precision and taped floor to ceiling. He raised his right eyebrow. "Like calendars much? You have a million of them."

He was exaggerating. There were only twelve; one for each year of my life since my mother ditched me. The fact I have each month (148 in total) individually tacked to my wall only makes it *look* like I have a million.

Cody got up from my bed and he walked to the wall. His eyes scanned the months. "Encryption?" He pointed to the number sequences I'd written in some of the boxes as a visible reminder that on occasion something good happens. "Wouldn't it be easier to have a diary like most girls?" He smiled.

I have a diary, but I wasn't going to admit it to Cody.

My dad gave it to me just a few weeks before we left Chicago. I was going through a tough spot at the time regarding the move. I know it sounds stupid, but I always held on to the hope that one day I'd see a woman who looked like me (only *way* cuter) in the produce aisle of the grocery store, or maybe walking towards me down the sidewalk, and there would be an instant connection. That she'd somehow know I was her daughter and she would immediately throw her arms around me while begging for forgiveness, which I'd give, but not before I somehow convinced her to become a homewrecker and kick Diane to the curb, so she—my real mom—could marry my dad, and we could all live happily-ever-after in Willa Fairytale Land.

It was my dad who suggested I write my diary entries to my birth mom instead of the standard "Dear Diary," which is dumb if you think about it—writing to an inanimate object instead of a real person. He said that way, if I ever did get a chance to meet her, I could give her the diary to read as the shortened Cliff Notes version of my life, instead of boring her with the long version.

Cody continued to review the calendars, his index finger following along the lines and the boxes. My numerical encryption wasn't all that sophisticated, but I don't think Cody knew what I'd written. At least I hoped he didn't.

This was bound to be one of my best memories on record—Cody in my room and touching my things—so I mentally took a detailed inventory of him.

Cody had changed out of his school clothes, a blue, red, and yellow plaid button-up short-sleeved shirt and khaki shorts, and he now wore a gray-and-black Rip Curl pullover hoodie and straight-leg black jeans. (Only in Southern California are shorts standard school-attire for boys and jeans considered their "after-school" clothes.)

I still wore the same thing I'd sweated in all day: Olivia's blue shirt and my jeans.

I pushed aside the papers on my desk to make workspace for Cody and opened my math book, turning to this week's lesson, my sweaty fingers sticking to the pages.

Cody continued his exploration of the calendars, his lips moving as if he were reading the entries, which of course he couldn't, because like I said, they are number coded. His eyes stopped on one of my earlier calendars, the one from the year I was four, and his face momentarily changed to … I don't know … not sadness, but something close to it. He brought his hand back to this year's calendar, and his face corrected, settling back into a smile as he double tapped an entry with his finger. In three strides, he was over at my desk and turning the chair around so he could straddle it.

"You think I'm cute, huh?" Cody asked, the dimple on his cheek adorable.

"Who told you I said that!" I gasped.

"Thursday, May 16th of this year. You said I'm the cutest guy you've ever seen." He smiled and crossed his arms on the top of the chair. "*Chicago …*" he drawled out. "Do you really L-O-V-E me? Cause if you do, we may be rushing things a bit. We might have to slow things down." Cody leaned the chair forward on two legs, enjoying this way too much.

"*How … what …*" I stammered, my eyes bugging out of my head while I wished for one of those California earthquakes I'd heard about, the kind so massive the ground opens and swallows your house whole.

Cody righted his chair to all four legs. "First day you attended Triton, May 16. '*Cody Cassidy is the cutest guy I've ever seen,*'" he repeated my entry word for word and spoke in falsetto. "You probably would have used an exclamation point, but the simple number code you used doesn't have a numerical equivalent," he joked.

I dropped my head to my desk and covered my head with my arms.

Cody peeled my arms back, his touch almost exploding my racing heart. "I told you I was a numbers guy. And hey, it's not like you used a tough one. Using 1 for an A, and 2 for a B, etcetera, is not exactly rocket science. The least you could have done was use the numbers in reverse and started with twenty-six. Just who are you trying to fool with your trickery?" He chuckled.

"My sister." The words sounded more like a moan.

"Oh, yeah ... that's right." Cody snapped his fingers. "The hot new girl in town. The cheerleader. The Gigi Hadid look-alike according to Dakota's brother."

"That's her." My voice cracked.

Cody reached across my desk and picked up a framed picture next to my computer. It was one of my dad and me and we were at Disneyland wearing matching mouse hats and sitting in an oversized teacup. "Is this your dad?"

The way Cody was staring at me, I got the feeling he knew the real answer to his question.

Cody twisted slightly and scooted his chair an inch closer to me so that we were shoulder to shoulder. "You were adopted. Weren't you, Chicago?" Cody's voice was just above a whisper. He twisted in the chair and pointed to the calendar from eight years ago taped to the wall behind us. "June 17th," he said before adding, "*the happiest day of your life,*" and decoding my inscription.

It's as if Cody had hit the Play button on a recorder as it all rushed back to me: the stifling heat of the day and not yet summer; the dress I wore: navy blue cotton with white stitching—the starch of the fabric scratchy on my skin. I saw in detail the smooth paneling of the wood on the walls of the courtroom—the swirling knots I thought resembled snail shells. I could even smell the leather of the chairs and the waxy lemon scent of the wood polish.

But what hit me like a punch to the gut were the *feelings.* The nervousness. The excitement. How I felt dizzy as I sat next to Dr. Shisbey, my new dad, while Diane, his wife and my new "mom," was away visiting her own mother in Ohio. Not that her absence made the adoption any less official, because

Diane had already signed off on it.

I remember I was so happy that day. *Crazy* happy. I was finally out of the Children's Home Society, away from the sad kids no one wanted, the leftovers and the less-than-perfect. I was a kid on top of the world. I had a better-looking face, one my dad helped to fix, and I had a new family. An honest to goodness real family.

Looking back, I should have set the bar lower regarding my expectations of happiness.

"Has it been tough, Chicago? Was it hard to adjust to living with a family you didn't know?" Cody's voice was low, as if the subject was something to speak about in whispers. He reached into his sweatshirt and pulled out a pack of gum. He offered me the pack before taking a stick for himself.

I gave a laugh that sounded more like a croak. "Look at this room." I pointed to the precision of the lined calendars on my wall and the meticulously organized bookshelves housing my books by spine color and height.

I went to my dresser and opened my drawers to reveal perfectly folded clothes and socks rolled tight and aligned in rows by pattern. Crossing to my closet, I slid open the door and exposed dozens of identical blue plastic tackle boxes and four pairs of the exact same shoes toeing a strip of masking tape I'd attached to the floor so my shoes would align.

"Has it been tough?" I repeated, holding his gaze. "What do *you* think, Cody? Does this look normal to you?"

Cody got up from the chair and came over to my closet. He pushed a few hangers to the side, every shirt parallel to the one next to it, and shook his head in disbelief while I cringed. If Cody told the other kids that I was an OCD neatnik with a calendar obsession, I'd be doomed for life. Maybe my dad would let me be homeschooled.

"Lures?" Cody asked, pointing to the tackle boxes. "Are all those boxes filled with fishing lures? Chicago, I wouldn't have thought of you as the outdoorsy type."

I shook my head no and breathed a sigh of relief. Cody wasn't freaked out by my cleanliness. At least I don't think he was. He was just amazed at how one closet could hold so many tackle boxes.

"Novelty erasers." I began to slide the mirrored

door closed.

Cody slid his foot on the track to keep the door open. "Wow!" He gave a loud whistle. "That's a lot of erasers. How many are in here?"

"At last count, 4,437, and none of them duplicates," I bragged. "It sounds like a lot, I know, but it's not even close to the world record. The record belongs to Petra Engels of Germany. She has 19,571 erasers, but then she's been collecting them since 1981. Petra's thirty-four now." I pushed my glasses towards the bridge of my nose. "Personally, I think thirty-four is way too old to be collecting erasers."

According to Olivia, six is too old to be collecting erasers, but I didn't say that to Cody.

Cody slid the closet door closed. "You're a regular eraser aficionado."

"I *was* a serious collector. But I've since kicked the habit with the help of those weekly meetings."

I was kidding. About the weekly meetings, not the part about being a serious collector.

The truth is, Diane has recently put the kibosh on my collecting saying if I was going to collect things the least I could do was collect something that would grow in value. Then she suggested stamps. (Yes, stamps — the soon-to-be-extinct dinosaurs of the postal service.)

We walked back to my desk and Cody adjusted our chairs so we could get to work. "Music?" he asked, turning up the volume on my computer speaker.

"No, thanks. I study better without it."

Cody laughed. "That might be part of the problem, Chicago. The right music might help. But, no worries. I'll talk instead. I know how much you like to listen to the sound of my voice. *Tuesday, September 5th.*" He pointed to this year's calendar.

I groaned, wanting to rip those darn calendars right off my walls. Cody grinned and began to organize my papers and notes before sharpening two pencils with my electric sharpener.

"Cody?"

"Yeah, Chicago?"

"You won't tell anybody about me, will you? About me being adopted and the weird stuff I do."

"Not if you don't want me to."

"I don't. Promise?"

Cody didn't answer me. Instead, he got up from his chair and walked over to the month of September. Licking the tip of his pencil, he scratched some numbers in today's square.

9-161815139195-2015-115516-3813171519-19531852019-3-311820518

He came back over and sat down. And then, just in case I was too clueless to understand my own code, he defiled my math book by ripping out the last page. It was a reference page, so no biggie, although now I'd probably have to pay for the book.

Cody wrote in big letters diagonally across the page: *I promise to keep Chicago's secrets. C. Cassidy.*

"We all good now?" Cody rubbed his hands together in that way people do when they're ready to get down to business.

"We're better than good. We're great!"

CHAPTER 6

I sat at the lunch table with Marley who was rocking the rainbow in lime-green shorts and a white, green, and orangey-yellow short-sleeved top. She wore little girls' canvas shoes with iridescent-pink sequins on them that resembled fish scales.

We still had fifteen minutes left of lunch and Marley was using it to hold court with the kids from *The Armada*. According to Marley *The Armada*, our school's paper, is recognized for its excellence and boasts a tagline that says, "Dedicated to moving things forward." Marley came up with it.

Our table included a veritable UN of kids from all over the world. The kids on the paper hailed from Iran, India, South Africa, and one of the "stans," … Krgyzstan? … Tajikistan? …

Uzbekistan?

Omar and Amir were having a debate (read: *argument*) about who-knows-what, because they are always arguing about something, and it's usually political or theological, and I *so* don't want to go there, and Marley was talking with the girls, Rebekka and Audrey, and using her standard, "There is no I in team," spiel, encouraging the girls to come up with creative new angles to upgrade the readership of the paper.

As the outsider in the group of outsiders (I'm not as smart as they are), and the only one not on the school paper (I couldn't get on), I listened while I stared across the lunch area at the cool kids laughing and joking and having fun instead of doing even more school work in their off time — just because.

From the distance of ten yards, Cody felt the strong pull of my gaze and he returned it, along with a wink and a wave.

Okay, that's not quite true, although he did glance my way. Accidentally.

Cody had to get up to throw his lunch into the

trash and the can was facing our table, so he had no other choice than to acknowledge me with a smile and a halfhearted wave. He may have actually winked at me, though. Then again, it had been a windy day and everyone had dirt and stuff caught in their eyes, so we were all going around winking and blinking and rubbing our eyes raw.

"How about you, Willa? Any ideas?" Marley interrupted my thoughts, tapping her pencil to her notebook. "We'd love a fresh perspective." She pushed some copies of the newspaper at me and I quickly scanned the pages.

I'm a fast reader, so in just under three minutes I'd finished, and I handed the pages back to her. "If you ask me, it's depressing." I shrugged in apology to the crew.

"Depressing? How so?" Marley wasn't the least bit mad. That's why Marley's such a great friend; she takes criticism well.

"Well ... it's like I'm watching the nightly news. It's all bad news without any good news to take away the sting." I opened to the second page and pointed to an article. "Here you talk about wanting zero tolerance for bullying. A definite need-to-know, and something I agree with a hundred percent, but still—depressing. And I'm sorry, but nowhere in the article does it address how to stop it, only that you're advocating zero tolerance."

"My bad," Audrey said. "That was my story."

My fingers dropped to another headline, "Killing With Cholesterol," a story about the cafeteria food. "Look here. Here's a story about the unhealthy foods served in our cafeteria. True? Yes. And not only depressing, but a story that just may land you a lawsuit from the School Board." I flipped open another edition of the paper and pointed to the front of the page. "And here is the story of a beached whale ... who *dies!*"

The kids all had some sort of epiphany expression and they nodded to one another.

"If you ask me," I said, my eyes going from face to face, "what your paper really needs is some humor."

The bell rang. I cleared my tray, shrugged on my backpack, and headed to class.

***

"I'm gonna kill you!" Olivia shouted at me as soon as she crossed the threshold, throwing her purse on the floor, the contents scattering like shrapnel. Her hair was messy and wild, and her skin was all splotchy and red.

I sat on the sofa in the living room watching television, the remote in my hand and still pointed at the set.

"So help me, Willa, I'm gonna get you for this, you stupid …"

I'm pretty sure what she yelled was the B word, but I cranked the volume up really high just as she said it and the noise of the television blasted, drowning out the word.

Olivia snatched the remote from my hands with her painted green talons, and pressed the mute button. "You're intentionally dressing me in the exact same clothes every day of every month! Aren't you, you brat!"

"I don't know what you're talking about." I said it calmly, but my insides were quaking.

She dropped to her knees and yanked some pictures out of her open purse. Clenching them in her hand, she thrust them in my face. "I'm wearing the same clothes in these pictures!" Her fist shook with rage.

I shrugged. The same? Compared to what?

"It so happens, *Willa Gene*," she sneered, "my class project for Psychology is titled *Sixty Days-Sixty Outfits*. I've had Denver take pictures of me every day for the past two months … with his iPhone!" I swallowed and blinked at her, not knowing what to say. "*Dates!*" she screamed at me, shaking the pictures in her hand in front of my glasses. "The camera has dates, you loser."

In my defense, now that I rethink what I originally thought was a foolproof plan—what kind of conceited, self-absorbed narcissist would have her boyfriend take a new picture of her, *every day*, for two entire months?

"You just wait," Olivia threatened, pointing her daggers at me. "I'll get you for this. If it's the last thing I do—I will get you, Willa."

***

"Marley! Where are you? Please, Marley! You have to call me back. It's an emergency!!"

I threw my phone across the room in frustration, where, thankfully, it landed on the cushioned comfort of my white shag carpet. Realizing the phone was now entirely out of my reach should Marley call me back, I got off my bed and went to get it.

My life was over. *Over!* Color me gone—over.

When Olivia said she was going to get back at me, she wasn't kidding. Which is why there were currently six girls—make that 6-6-6, *devil* girls—all in my family room spreading their sleeping bags on my living room floor in order to have a slumber party—with me—in exchange for the opportunity of a lifetime. (Or so said the Evite, the ridiculous, too-cute, make me gag invitation that Olivia e-mailed to them).

The invitation promised in return for suffering through a night in my presence, Olivia would reward them with a beauty makeover and give a short seminar on the latest fashion trends. *Olivia's Beauty Basics: Top 10 Must Haves*, the invitation promised, along with the date, the time, and MapQuest directions to our house.

I dialed another number. My dad answered on

the first ring. "Dad, it's Willa," I said.

"Sweetheart, I know your voice, and besides, your Facebook picture shows up on my screen," he said, chuckling. "What can I do for you?"

"Where are you?" With my phone still held to my ear, I quietly opened my door. Peeking my head out into the hallway, I could see my dad sitting on the counter stool in the kitchen and doing something that looked like shucking peas. I waved to him and then shut my door.

"Come out, Willa." My dad spoke into the phone, but I could have heard him anyway. "Who knows, you may actually have some fun."

Sure, a real blast. Even Diane said she felt a migraine coming on when the girls all arrived and she quickly ditched the festivities in order to go to the movies with friends.

"Dad, what are they doing now?" *Crowing incantations? Buffing their cauldron? Sticking pins in a tiny wax doll made of my likeness?* I started to hyperventilate and had to sit on the floor and put my head between my knees.

I heard a pea snap and my dad whispered, "I can't be sure, but it looks like Olivia and Blaine are taking turns plucking the girls' eyebrows. Or maybe they're applying false eyelashes, it's hard for me to see from where I'm standing. As far as I can tell, everyone seems to be having a good time."

The doorbell rang announcing the pizza.

"At least come and have some dinner, Willa. You can't stay in your room all night. That's not being a very good hostess."

But I wasn't the hostess! *I was the hostage.* I didn't invite those girls over and I didn't want them in my house. This was nothing but a vicious plan to get back at me.

"Wilhelmina …" my dad warned.

I plucked at the sleeve of my white long-sleeved shirt. I didn't want to press my luck with Olivia, so I had to go back to wearing my own clothes, and it was white and plain. Just like me.

"Fine!" I said. "I'll go play nice. Maybe I'll ask them if they want to play some pin the tail on Willa."

I stuck my phone in my pocket and gave in to the temptation of pepperoni.

CHAPTER 7

I admit, it wasn't going too badly. In fact, it was going too *well*. Slasher-movie too well, with all the girls primping and laughing and having a good time, except for me, who sat in the corner, alone. Any minute I expected the front door to throw open and find Freddy, or Jason, or Billy, or Jester force his way into the room and hack all of us to death in little pieces—a standard outcome in mainstream slasher cinema when things are going far too well to be considered normal.

"Who's next?" Olivia asked in some perky voice she must have borrowed. She flexed her tweezers.

So far, Olivia—and Blaine, who was spending the night to help Olivia with the party—had tweezed and shaped the brows of Dakota, Dallas,

Hallie, Keiran, and Kirby. Brylee declined, saying she would need her mom's permission first.

"I think Willa should go next," Dakota said, sipping on her soda through a straw so she wouldn't ruin her lip gloss. "But tweezers won't be enough. You may need to get out the weed whacker."

"Oh, *sis*," Olivia said, laughing and trying to earn points with her potential future sister-in-law by pretending that Dakota was as cute as the dickens.

Olivia came toward me with evil intent in her eyes, but to give her credit, she looked really pretty while she did it, in her off-the-shoulder electric-blue silk blouse and her white skinny jeans.

"No way," I said. I tucked my legs underneath me and tried to curl up like a roly-poly for protection.

"*Will-a! Will-a! Will-a!*" the girls all started chanting. They even stood up to yell, and Dallas was so exuberant she accidentally spilled her root beer all over Diane's beige sofa.

I wasn't getting out of it. Not unless I called my dad on my cell phone and told him I was having an appendicitis attack. Or maybe periodontal disease.

"Okay!" I said, uncoiling myself and going over to the *beauty parlor* chair—Olivia's red upholstered desk chair she'd wheeled into the family room. "Fine. You all win. But I want Blaine to do it." I pointed at Blaine and she nodded yes while licking the pizza grease off her fingers.

"Cat-a-pillar! Cat-a-pillar!" Dakota chanted, referring to my eyebrows, but it didn't catch on, so she stopped.

Five minutes later, swollen and pink and plucked like a chicken, I squinted in the mirror at my reflection. If you didn't count the swelling and the little bit of blood dotted just under my newly tweezed eyebrows, I didn't look half-bad. In fact, I looked pretty good.

"Wow, Willa," Kirby said, tipping her head to the side and twisting her long blonde hair around the length of her finger. "With your eyebrows tweezed and without your glasses, you're almost kinda cute." And Blaine agreed, adding I looked a little like the teen actress Bailee Madison on *Good Witch*, which was a major stretch but a nice compliment. Then negating the compliment by adding, "But the young Bailee, when she still had that chubby face."

Olivia's eyes tightened and she glared at them. I got the feeling this was not what Olivia had in mind when she wanted to play dress-up—me getting some of the attention. I'm pretty sure the night was supposed to be all about Olivia. She glanced over at the built-in bookcases lining the opposite wall of the room, a strange light filling her eyes.

Olivia started to purr. "If you think Willa is cute now, you should see the pictures of how cute she was as a baby."

"Olivia, no!" I gasped, horrified, and realizing her intent. "Please, Olivia, no. I *beg* you! Not my baby pictures," I pleaded, my voice wavering while sweat started to bead at the back of my neck. "*No*, Olivia."

But Olivia, the Velociraptor, had a plan. A mean and vicious plan. And before I could stop her, she sprinted across the room and pulled open the bottom cupboard, grabbing my baby book from the second shelf. She cracked open the pages and swiftly peeled off the pictures, quickly passing them to the girls as if they were discount coupons at the mall to Abercrombie & Fitch.

All eyes grew wide in horror as they stared at the pictures. There were gasps and mouths covered with hands. Someone said "Eww," and Brylee had to turn her head away.

They were the pictures of me—before my surgery.

The pictures showed a homely toddler, with one lazy eye that pointed in, behind green plastic glasses held to her face by an elastic band, and with a visible cleft that ran from lip to nostril. And it's not as if I was missing the bottom half of my face, the way some kids look before their clefts or palates are repaired, but the cleft was gaping and pink and glistened with my saliva, and my lips pulled sideways in a lopsided grin, revealing those teeth, as pointed as a poodle's.

"I hate you!" I screamed at Olivia, stumbling over the leather ottoman in my attempt to escape, hot tears stinging my eyes. "You deserve each other!" I cried, pointing to Dakota and Olivia, and lumping Dallas in with them. I ran from the room—to my father.

"Willa!" Blaine called out to me and at least having the decency to appear mortified at her friend's behavior. "It's okay, Willa! You look better. You even look *good* ... now."

But it didn't help.

I stumbled into the kitchen and over to the counter. "Dad!" I pleaded. "Can I homeschool? Please, Dad?" I tugged hard on his arm, spilling the peas. Seeing my tears, he stopped his shelling and drew me tightly to his chest in a hug. "I can't go back to school, Dad. Not now. Not when all the girls have seen what I looked like before my surgery. Please, Dad. Please don't make me go." My tears dripped down the front of his shirt.

"Olivia Rose! Get in here!" Dad roared over my head, the force of it reverberating through his chest. Olivia skulked into the room, her blue blouse sagging off her shoulder.

Olivia dropped her head in shame. "Dad ... I ..." She didn't finish.

My dad released me and took a step back. Reaching inside his pocket, he pulled out his handkerchief, handing it to me so I could wipe my runny nose.

"You're grounded for two weeks, miss," he said to Olivia. "No car. And no phone. Now hand it over." He held out his hand with his palm up.

"No, Dad! Not my *phone*," she wailed.

"Now, Olivia!"

With difficulty, Olivia dug her phone out of the back pocket of her tight jeans while giving me the stink eye. Olivia's phone was her life. She continued to glower and she shook her head at me as if it were my fault she lost her connection to the world.

My dad put the colander in the sink and neatly folded the kitchen towel. "I think this party is over. Olivia, tell the girls to let their parents know I'll be driving them home. Willa, come and say good-bye to the girls."

With the way my dad said it, using his, *I'm the dad and I'm the boss* voice, I knew it was a command and not a request. I gave Olivia a head start so she could go into the family room first to break the news, but by then the girls had already started to fold their sleeping bags and gather their things, so they pretty much knew the party was over.

"Bye, Willa," Kirby said, followed by Dallas and Hallie, when my dad stood ready by the front door, with the minivan keys in his hand.

Olivia came ambling down the hallway from the direction of her bedroom, humming, and clearly hiding something behind her back. "Oh, *Willa ...*" she sang, and it was obvious she was up to no good.

All eyes were on her while the girls lined up at the front door with Dakota and Dallas closest to me and holding up the rear. Olivia triumphantly whipped the hidden item from behind her back, holding it up high, where it dangled from her claws.

"Willa, isn't this Cody's hat? Maybe Dakota can give it back to him." We both glanced over at Dakota who stood shocked, all the color suddenly draining from her face. "It seems he must have left it behind in your *bedroom.*"

CHAPTER 8

"It was terrible!" I complained to Marley as we walked to school on the Monday after the party that wasn't. "The worst day of my life. *Ever!*" And with my H-SAM, it was a day I'd continue to relive a billion times over. "Really, Mar. The absolute *worst.*"

I rolled up the sleeves of my shirt because I was starting to get warm. I'd gone out of the box and wore a black plaid one today instead of my solid white, a boy's shirt my dad bought for me at the surf shop. A present, he said, for surviving my ordeal.

"I'm so sorry, Willa. I would have called you back if I could." Marley trotted along on her Gap Girls pink jelly shoes with the oversized hibiscus glued to the tops. "But I was with my mom visiting the kids on the pediatric ward of her hospital and I didn't have cell service."

"It was a train wreck. A *total* train wreck," I continued, adjusting my backpack higher up on my shoulders. "You should have seen the look on their faces when Olivia handed them the pictures. They were all grossed out. I swear, I thought Brylee was going to puke." I kicked an old newspaper to the gutter and then went to retrieve it when I saw Marley frown. I picked it up and put it in someone's blue recycle bin parked at the curb.

"No homeschool then?" Marley asked, appearing relieved.

I bent down to pick up an empty plastic water bottle and I went to toss it in the next recycling bin three houses down from the last. "No. My dad said his workload is too busy, and Diane says she's finally starting to get the hang of hot yoga. Besides, my dad said he didn't raise a quitter." (He did, he just doesn't want to admit it.)

We arrived at school, two more dolphins in a sea of them—we're called The Triton Dolphins— Marley smiling and nodding to the kids as we walked by. They did the same to her. Quirky or not, it was hard not to like Marley.

"There she is," I heard someone whisper behind my back. "That's her! That's the girl in those gross pictures."

A sudden roaring erupted in my head and my mouth went dry as a horrible suspicion washed over me. The hairs on my arm raised and my palms suddenly started to itch.

Marley and I rounded the corner and entered the main hall of the campus, where more kids whispered and some pointed, nodding and shaking their heads, a few using their fingers to pull their lips apart to make ugly faces. My steps slowed down, my feet leaden, and sweat began to ooze from my pores. We entered the hallway where our lockers were. Mine wasn't hard to find, it was the one with a crowd.

I took one look at my locker and felt my world start to slide.

My pictures! Copies of my pictures blown up and taped to my locker, helter skelter, like grotesque pieces of an oversized puzzle. And not only were the pictures of me, but of other children, too. Third World children with severe cleft palates, their sad faces split at the middle, terribly disfigured, and looking mangled and maimed.

Marley sprang into action, pushing her way through the crowd. She started ripping down the pictures, the ones she could reach, stuffing them inside her book bag, and trying to jump to get at the ones over her head. Up and down she jumped, grabbing and stuffing, her face fierce with determination.

"Willa Shisbey, boyfriend stealer" someone had scrawled in red lipstick smeared like blood across my face on the picture up top that Marley couldn't reach. And it didn't take much to figure out who was behind it.

The crowd continued to grow; kids I knew, kids I didn't, laughing and pointing, making mean comments and terrible faces, and still I stayed frozen, too shocked to move. It could have been two minutes or two years, while Marley did her best to remove the pictures, jumping up again and again to tear them all down. She'd done her best, but a single one remained, a picture of me, my eye crossed and my lip split, taped far too high for her to reach.

"I'll get it." Cody soundlessly came from behind and easily reached up to remove the picture. He held it in his hands, his expression soft with sympathy, looking from Marley to me, and not quite sure who to hand the picture to.

Marley took it from him and added it to the others in her overfilled bag.

And still I stood paralyzed, while the sound of some far-off wind roared in my head, and despair darkened my vision, my body going numb with my pain.

"Come with me," Marley commanded, taking my hand and pulling me down the hallway toward the journalism room. I started to collapse.

"I'll help," Cody told Marley, supporting me on the other side while we walked, his jaw clenched and looking like he wanted to hit something.

The first bell rang and kids started to shuffle off to class, still laughing and hooting and making those terrible faces.

"Thanks, Cody. I'll take it from here," Marley

said, and although I was still dazed, my mind registered she'd probably heard that line before from her mother. Cody nodded and left the room just as her teacher arrived.

The Armada kids started to filter in the room, sneaking glances our way, but leaving us alone. Marley's journalism teacher, Mr. Snyder, told the kids to get started while he left the room to get some supplies.

"You're not giving up, Willa! I won't let you. *'The harder the conflict, the more glorious the triumph.'* Thomas Paine," she quoted, while organizing her supplies.

I still hadn't said a word.

"Give me your wrist," she instructed. I held my arm out, and Marley pushed up my sleeve. "Ordinarily, I'm not a fan of body art," she said, sizing up the diameter of my wrist, "but desperate times call for desperate measures, and besides this won't be permanent."

Marley reached inside her book bag and pulled a fine-line Sharpie from inside. Quickly, but artistically, she drew on my wrist her rendition of me as Spider-girl, complete with web and cape. She tugged down my sleeve and buttoned my button.

"Maybe you better wear your sweatshirt in gym class. I don't want to get you in trouble."

I still hadn't found my voice. For once in my life, there were no words floating around in my head waiting to be expressed. No vowels. No consonants to form the syllables to create a sentence. *Nothing* ...

"You're in shock right now. But you'll get through this, Willa. I promise. It's terrible. It's hurtful, I know. But it's not the end of the world." Marley patted my knee and I noticed her glitter polish was peeling. "The kids I saw this weekend at the hospital, Willa, ... *those* kids have it tough. Those kids are *dying*, Willa. Sweet little angels with leukemia, and lymphoma, bone cancer, and neuroblastoma—a cancer in *babies*."

The second bell rang and I knew I was going to be tardy to first period. Who cared? My world had stopped spinning. What's another tardy in relationship to the Apocalypse?

***

And my day went by quietly. Sounds were muted—for real, or imagined. The snickers stopped, although most of the kids wouldn't look at me and they dropped their eyes as I walked by. Except for Dakota, who lifted her nose in the air and flicked her hair while grabbing tightly to Cody's arm, which he immediately pulled away. He even walked in the opposite direction, in order to put some distance between them.

I didn't talk much to anyone at our table during lunch. Maybe a yes or a no, only half listening when Marley mentioned we had a new boy in school, and told the group he was over at the Friendship Bench, and who wanted to be the first one to welcome him?

"Why don't you go, Willa?" Marley softly said, while I kept my head down and traced the lines of her drawing on the inside of my arm with my finger. "It may do you some good."

"Sure." I sighed, slowly swinging my legs over the bench seat, figuring it was the least I could do because Marley had come to *my* rescue my first day at Triton. She had proved to be a wonderful friend and it was only right I should do the same in an effort to pay it forward, like she says.

The boy sat by himself, not that he was alone, exactly, because a noon aide was standing by his side looking like she'd rather be picking up rotten apple cores from underneath the lunch tables than to be standing next to the kid in the motorized wheelchair. The boy seemed to be around our age, although he was small for his age, and his body twitched and jerked, his neck twisting from side to side, while a line of drool dribbled from his mouth.

That he could have used a hand, some help to wipe his chin, must not have occurred to the aide. Or maybe it had, but she wasn't wearing her trash pick-up gloves, and so maybe she was afraid to touch the boy without them. Silly lady.

"Hi, I'm Willa," I said, reaching out to take the boy's curled hand in mine to shake it, his hand cold in my warm one.

"Um 'awbby," he mumbled, his arms flailing around a little, his freckled face lighting in a crooked smile while saliva dribbled down his chin.

I waited for the noon aide to help. When she didn't, I stared her down. She shrugged and gave a look that said she didn't get paid to wipe; trash was more her thing. I dug around inside my backpack to search for a tissue. "May I?" I asked him, dabbing only after he gave me the okay. I tucked the tissue in his front pocket for later. "I'm sorry. Was that Bobby, or Robbie?"

I'd learned in the orphanage, with the kids with cerebral palsy (CP) that it sometimes takes a second try. I also learned they often jerked and that sometimes they drooled. But hey, who doesn't? My pillow is wet every morning.

"Mm …waa …bee," he said, taking the time to enunciate the words.

"Robbie?" Robbie nodded yes. "Got it. And your last name is …?" As a time saver, I read Robbie's printed school schedule taped to the tray on his wheelchair. "Wise," I read aloud. "A smart guy, huh? I knew it. One of the intelligent, quiet types. Not me, I'm the dumb, obnoxious type." I smiled at him.

"Don't believe a word she says," Cody said, suddenly standing beside me, where he'd arrived silent as a snail, and nudging me with his shoulder. "Girl's got a memory like a steel trap." Cody tapped his finger to his temple, his head covered in a knitted orange beanie. "Although her math skills are a little shaky." He nudged me again. "Welcome to

Triton, dude. *Cody Cassidy*—surfer, skater, and all around rock star," he joked, introducing himself to Robbie and balling his hand to give Robbie a fist bump.

Robbie's head strained to the right and he uttered a moan I took to mean, "Yeah!" or "Right on!" It takes me awhile, but I'm a pretty good CP translator. The CP kids were always the last to be adopted at the home, even behind the kids with Down syndrome, so I learned to develop a good ear for their dialect in all the time we spent together.

Cody pulled his hat off his head, his hair flattened, but still amazing. "I'm gonna let you in on a little secret." He leaned toward Robbie and placed his hat on Robbie's head, tugging it down so it almost covered one eye. "To earn respect around this place, you gotta be a rebel."

"Web … al!" Robbie crowed.

I knew Cody was only being nice because he felt sorry for me. Sorry his hideous cretin of a girlfriend was bent on destroying my life. But I didn't care, because it felt so good to be warmed by Cody's presence, to be infected with his bright smile, and his easy way with people.

Cody probably wouldn't have gone out of his way to befriend Robbie it if weren't for what happened today. Cool kids don't need to take a stand, but if Robbie was getting some pity acknowledgment because of what happened today at my locker, it was all right by me.

The noon aide had wandered over to pick up some empty trays and spilled milk cartons that littered the lunch area, like the flotsam and the jetsam (that's shipwreck stuff) of the sea. She shuffled back over on her rubber-soled shoes when the bell rang, ready to help Robbie get to his next class.

Cody tucked his hands inside his jean pockets and he spoke to Robbie, who continued to smile and only occasionally shake, visibly happy to be noticed. "And just in case you get any ideas about this one here," he said, jerking his head to the side twice to mean me, "just know I'll be watching you. Because I happen to have it on good authority …" he paused to look my way, "she L-O-V-E—loves me."

CHAPTER 9

"Concentrate, Chicago."

"I am."

"I mean on the problem. I see you staring at me," Cody said, his head dipped over the math book as we studied at his house. Maybe four-eyes needed to be Cody's new nickname. He seemed to be on to me.

The carpets were being shampooed over at my house in preparation for Diane's monthly Bunco party, so Cody was tutoring me at his house. And what a house! Cody and his family lived on the water in Huntington Harbor. That's what happens when your dad owns burger joints with a gold and red sign that says "Billions and Billions Served" and boasts having the ninetieth largest economy in the world.

The house sat on a street with other mansion-looking houses. "Overbuilt and ostentatious" is how Cody described it when he gave me the directions, and looking like it belonged more in Tuscany, Italy than in Orange County, California. It had a big black iron electric gate with double Cs forged into the iron, and they opened when Cody buzzed me through. The letters stood for Craig and Christina, Cody said, his parents, who have an obsession for names beginning with C.

The driveway was long, about a mile it felt like, but probably not more than the length of half a football field, and it led to a two-story house with huge black doors and an iron doorknocker made to look like … want to guess? … two Cs! Inside, it was pretty cool, with large open spaces littered with boy stuff and all kinds of different boards: skateboards, boogie boards, surfboards. Cody said they had snowboards too, but they were in rafters in the garage somewhere, although the best ones were at their house in the mountains.

The whole backside of the house had these huge windows that looked out over the water, the back harbor of Huntington Beach, Cody explained, and they had a dock with a boat in the slip. But this wasn't like a little boat or anything. It was a huge boat! Cody explained it's actually called a yacht and that it had two bedrooms below deck and a full kitchen and everything.

The yacht wasn't theirs, Cody said, only the dock. They sold their boat a couple years ago because his dad said it didn't make sense to waste money maintaining a boat with a family too busy to use it. Now they rented the slip to some friends who lived inland.

"What? No helicopter?" I asked after Cody had given me the grand tour, including the four-car garage, where his dad kept his sports cars.

"Naw. My dad usually rents one if he needs it."

I thought Cody was kidding, but he wasn't. "Seriously? *Your dad flies around in a helicopter?*" And here I thought it was a big deal when my dad got us a new minivan with a DVD player in the back seat.

Cody dug his hands deeper in the center pocket of his black-striped hoodie. He grinned. "Not for work, Chicago. We don't have *that* much money."

Cody laughed, and the sound echoed off those tall walls. "It's for snow skiing. The helicopter drops him off on the top of the mountain and then he skis down it. But usually he shares the cost with other people, because my dad can be a tight wad."

The front door burst open and Cody's older brother jogged through it, excited and out of breath. At least I assumed it was his brother, because the guy looked a lot like Cody, only he was the taller and more mature-looking version. Probably the lead singer of the family boy band would be my guess. He wore white-and-black plaid board shorts, a black Hobie tee, and white sunglasses pushed back on his blond head.

"He did it!" he exclaimed. "He got totally tubed! Dude finally got tubed. We used his short board. Honestly, man, the dog was awesome."

Dude? Man? Dog? I wasn't following. But Cody knew exactly what he meant and he yelled, "Right on!" He raised his hand and gave the guy a high five, just as another boy—the youngest member of the band—a kid around ten, who probably sang back up, came through the door followed by a small, dripping wet, white-and-brown dog. The dog ran into the room like a rocket and then promptly shook, leaving water and sand all over Mrs. Cassidy's hardwood floors.

The lead singer noticed me, and he held out his hand to shake. "I'm Carter," he said, "and that's Connor." He hitched his shoulder to the right where Connor stood shyly, now holding the dog in his arms. Connor shyly said hi before dropping his eyes to the floor. Taking the dog from his brother, Carter said, "And this is Dude, the wonder dog. He just tasted his first barrel. I got it on my phone and everything! YouTube, buddy," he said to Cody, digging his phone out of his pocket and waving it up in the air.

Mansions? Yachts? Helicopters? *Surfing dogs* …? California was a very strange place, for sure.

"Your dog surfs," I said, and it wasn't a question. I mean, yeah, of course it was only natural the dog should surf. He was a Cassidy.

"He skateboards, too," Cody said. "Connor, go get his board," he told his little brother, reaching out his hand to scratch Dude under his ear. The dog may have been a surfing savant, but he kinda smelled.

A minute later, Connor rode into the hallway—which was half the width of my entire house—on a skateboard. He rolled to a stop in front of us and then got off. Immediately Dude jumped on top, looking up at Cody awaiting further instructions.

"Watch this," he told me. "Go, Dude!" he commanded, stretching his arm and pointing.

And I'll be darned if that little dog didn't start using his front paw to propel himself forward and gain speed before balancing all four paws on the skateboard and rolling down the entire length of the hallway, where it ended at the kitchen. Once there, he jumped off, used his nose to turn the board in the direction facing us, and then he started our way, rolling joyfully along, just as the door to the garage opened and Mrs. Cassidy walked through it, her arms full of groceries.

"Boys! How many times have I told you I don't want that dog skateboarding in the house! He's ruining all my expensive wood floors."

Dude knew he was busted and he jumped off his skateboard. Cody took the board from him while

Carter tried to fix a scuffmark with his flip-flop. Dude, knowing he was in deep doo, dog or otherwise, ran from the room, probably to hide under a bed as a normal dog would.

"Sorry," Mrs. Cassidy apologized, when she noticed me standing there. "I'm not usually such a witch, but we just had all the floors refinished. For the *second* time," she emphasized while frowning at her sons. "And my husband says if he has to do it again, we're sending all the boys off to boarding school and he's euthanizing the dog."

"Mom!" Connor gasped.

"Kidding ..." Mrs. Cassidy said, heading off to the kitchen. "*I'm kidding ...*" she sing-songed. "About the dog," she called out over her shoulder. "Not the boarding school!"

"Mom, Willa's here to tutor me in math!" Cody yelled out to his mother, who from the sounds of things was putting the groceries away in the cupboards. I gave him a strange look but didn't say anything. "We'll be upstairs in my room." Cody started heading up the stairs while his brothers went into the "family room" (a movie theater, if you ask me) and turned on the big screen, the surround sound reverberating through the walls.

"Okay, but remember to leave the door open," she called back. It must be a parent thing.

"So," I said to Cody, once we settled in the chairs at his desk—some glass and chrome thing that held a desktop Mac computer and a laptop, besides. "I'm here to tutor *you*, huh? Then it looks like you can count out a four-year college and start looking for a good two-year community college, instead."

Cody booted up his desktop, not meeting my gaze. "Uh, yeah, about that ..." The computer blazed to life, his screensaver a picture of Dude riding a wave and wearing a big dog grin on his face and black sunglasses, a wet scarf sagging at his neck. "It's kind of a long story, and one I don't know if I want to get into right now."

We all have our secrets and if Cody didn't want to share his, who was I to judge?

"No problem."

"Thanks." Cody nodded at me, and then he squinted, scrutinizing my face. "Is there something different about you?"

"What do you mean?"

"Did you shave your eyebrows?" He pointed in the general direction of my eyes. "They were bushier before."

Well, thanks, there, Cody. How nice of you to point that out.

"Not *shaved.* They were tweezed, to give me a gentle arch—according to my sister's friend, Blaine. And not something I would necessarily recommend. It hurt like heck."

"I'll try and remember that," Cody said, smiling. If I had more guts I would have asked Cody if he liked them.

Cody opened his math book, his arm accidentally touching mine and sending sparks even through the cotton of my long-sleeved shirt. It wasn't a button-up shirt, for a change, but instead, a long red tee. I may not have been a total babe in the fashion world; but at least I'd gotten out of the box enough to ditch my white button-down shirt and try to introduce some color to my wardrobe.

Cody seemed unaffected by the touch, and he read the first problem. "Solve the equation, if possible, $3(2x - 5) + 4(x - 2) = 12$."

I stared at Cody, my chin resting on my hands, mesmerized by his profile and the sound of his voice.

Cody pushed the book closer to me, bringing me back to the present. I dropped my eyes to the page and saw nothing but a bunch of black numbers. And some story problems about the depth of water in a pool that had just sprung a leak.

"Go ahead," he said and tapped his pencil to the page with the tip of his eraser. "You try to solve it first."

It may as well have been written in Greek. Which now that I think about it, it was, since the Greeks invented geometry.

I stabbed at the problem with my finger. "Look here! 'Solve the equation, *if possible*,'" I read. "If possible! Right there the book is telling us the outcome is in doubt." I shook my head with frustration. "I don't know why I'm so dumb. I feel like I'm in third grade again, and it's that fourth

Wednesday in April—the 22nd—the day I wore that stupid dress Olivia told me was adorable, when it totally wasn't. In fact, it was an absolute horror, and it had these stupid little cats printed on it in blue and pink. Plus, it was thirty-five degrees outside and I was freezing," I rambled on, remembering the day clearly.

"I had Cocoa Pebbles for breakfast … Anyway, we had this dumb test, and I got majorly stumped on question number five. 'Mark is going on a walk-a-thon,'" I said in a high voice. "'For every ½ mile he walks, Mark gets 75 cents. When he finished his walk, Mark raised $3.75. How far did Mark walk?' It was like the woodchuck story, only with Mark!"

Cody stared at me as if I'd grown horns on my head, his eyes wide.

"You know …" I tried to explain. "The question seemed as impossible to answer as 'how much wood would a woodchuck chuck if a woodchuck could chuck wood'? Only with Mark and his quarters instead."

Cody's fingers started to fly across the keyboard, and there was an odd expression on his face. "What was the weather in Chicago, March 13, 2007?"

"Seventy-four degrees," I answered easily.

And so it went that way for a minute or two, Cody's fingers skimming across the keyboard and me playing weather girl, Cody amazed at my "talent," as he called it.

"Boston, April 20th, 2009."

"Fifty-one degrees and partly cloudy. And the only reason I know that is because I heard it on the news. It was the same day as the Boston Marathon, and a guy from Ethiopia won it—Deriba Merga—with a time of about thirty minutes, I think." I didn't know for sure. The news bores me. By then I'd left the room and went to the kitchen to have a peanut butter and jelly sandwich.

Cody shook his head as if he didn't believe it. Not about Deriba's finish time. For sure he didn't believe that. Nor should he. It might be impossible to run a marathon that quick. Aren't marathons twenty-six miles or something?

"*How* ... *What* ..." Cody sputtered, trying to wrap his mind around it. He got up from his chair and started pacing back and forth, shaking his head.

I sighed, that familiar feel of alienation coming on strong—the glass wall going up that separates me from the rest of the world.

I bent my head and rubbed my temples with my thumbs. The last of my secrets had finally been revealed. Cody now knew I was adopted by the Shisbeys. And he'd seen the pictures of me, the proof that I was born with a messed-up face. What difference would it make to give him one more reason why I'm such a freak? I patted Cody's empty seat. He returned and sat down beside me.

Cody sat down, continuing to stare. "You really remember all of that stuff? Chicago, man, that's amazing. I can't remember what I had for breakfast yesterday, let alone on some random day five years ago."

I didn't answer right away. Instead, I started doodling on my paper, drawing stars down the margin. Cody pulled the pencil from my hand.

I turned to face Cody. He knew everything else about me; he may as well know the rest. "Have you ever heard of something called H-SAM? Highly Superior Autobiographical Memory? Or Hyperthymesia?"

"Hyperthymesia? Isn't that what Poppy Montgomery's character, Carrie Wells, has on that series, *Unforgettable*?"

"Exactly. As well as the actress Marilu Henner, only she has it in real life."

I quickly typed Marilu's name on the keyboard and images of her smiling face filled the screen. "Marilu's documented as number twelve in the world and I'm number thirteen. Although since she came out with her book, now a ton of people claim to have it."

I watched Cody as he silently read her bio, his lips moving as he read. Cody stared at the screen and then back at me. His eyes were kinda bugged and his breathing was louder than normal, but on the upside, he didn't go screaming from the room.

"The thing with H-SAM is I can only remember stuff that relates to me personally," I explained. "I have to see it or experience it myself. H-SAM is a me-me-me, I-I-I affliction. In that sense, I'm a lot like Olivia, my sister. You know, only caring about what happens to me and nobody else?" I kidded, trying (unsuccessfully) to lighten the moment.

"It seems cool. Is it like a photographic memory?"

Cody leaned back in his desk chair and started spinning from side to side, eventually spinning in a complete circle before coming to a stop facing me, our knees touching.

"*Hardly*. Don't you think I'd be doing better in math if it were? H-SAM's not anything positive that helps with my life. In fact, it's the opposite. The exact opposite. Having H-SAM stinks."

"Why?" Cody asked, and then he snapped his fingers. "*Man!* ... If I had what you have, I'd be on TV. Oprah, maybe. Oh wait." He shook his head. "I don't think she's on anymore. Then *60 Minutes*, or *20/20*. You could be famous, Chicago! You could make a ton of money doing the publicity circuit. All the talk shows ... radio ... they could do a movie about you ..." he trailed off. Picking up two pencils, he started drumming the desk.

I gently closed the math book and started to tidy Cody's desk, my head down, my hair falling forward and hiding my face. Suddenly I didn't feel like studying. Didn't Cody see? I didn't want to be a freak. A weirdo. Someone whose name was in medical books. The thirteenth documented person in the whole world who would never be able to forget the bad moments of her life and the dark memories. There was no way to escape the things that make me sad.

Cody didn't know—nobody knows—that I'm constantly trying to block the bad memories of my life, or else be consumed by them.

I pulled one of the pencils out of his hand and set it down. "It sucks because I have to *feel* the bad stuff, Cody! Not just remember it, but also *feel* it, all over again, each time the memory comes back. Not once, as you do, where when you get hurt you only hurt then, and after, you forget the pain, where the scar is the only reminder that it ever happened. Cody, I …" I struggled to continue. "I have to live the hurt over and over again."

And I don't know why, but the memory of the day my mother left me came back right then, and it hit me like a bus. My breath caught and my heart hammered as I remembered the way the tears darkened my mother's light brown eyes that cold morning—eyes almost the same color as Cody's. I recalled the exact pattern of the knitted purple scarf she wore … and the sweet smell of flowers as she hugged me … her hand extending to ring the doorbell to the Children's Home Society of Chicago … the shrill sound of the doorbell ringing …

I remembered it all.

"Chicago," Cody said softly. He placed his right hand on top of mine. "I… Wow, I don't know what to say."

The first tear spilled down my cheek and then another. I accepted the crumpled tissue Cody pulled out of his pocket, briefly wondering if it had been used, and I wiped the tears from my face.

"You want to know how many times I've relived my mother leaving me at the orphanage because she thought I was too ugly to keep, Cody? Four thousand, two hundred, and twenty-five times. And that's only if I think about it once a day. The beach fiasco, with everyone making fun of me? The pictures of me on my locker? You know how many times …?" I couldn't go on.

"Hey, Chicago." Cody awkwardly pulled me to him in a hug, patting me on the back, enveloping me in the coconut smell of him. "Don't cry," he said, which made me cry harder. "It's okay, Chicago. Don't cry."

Cody let me go far too quickly, and we both sat in our embarrassment while I gathered my things and stuffed them inside my backpack. There wasn't going to be any more studying for the day.

"Is this a secret you want me to keep, Chicago? Because if it is, my lips are sealed." He locked his lips and threw the invisible key over his shoulder.

"If you don't mind, I'd appreciate it, Cody." I used the bottom of my shirt to wipe my face. "The kids think I'm enough of a weirdo without the word getting out I have H-SAM. I just want to pretend to be a normal kid who fits in. That's all, Cody. I just want to fit in."

CHAPTER 10

"He hugged me, Marley! Cody hugged me. Of course it was because I was crying my eyes out like a little baby, but if that's all it takes, I may have to cry more often," I told Marley as we sat on the benches during short recess. Marley wore a bright orange-and-white star print top, and white leggings. Her shoes were red metallic. She looked like a cute 50/50 bar. Except for the shoes. The shoes were *Wizard of Oz* all the way.

Marley seemed distracted. "Uhh … yeah, you were crying … that's great, Willa." Marley had her head down and she punched some numbers into her calculator.

I took off my glasses and polished the lenses. "You mean it's great that I was crying, or it's great that Cody hugged me?" For a genius, Marley can get easily distracted.

Marley snapped her head up, her pigtail dreadlocks bobbing. "I'm sorry, Willa. You were saying?"

What I hadn't yet said, but wanted to, was that I finally discovered the perk of having H-SAM. If you have a good memory, or in this case a *great* one, good events can be as easily recalled as all the bad ones. Until now, it was just all theory because my life was pretty sucky. But not anymore. Now I have something to hold onto. So far I've had the chance to relive Cody's hug about a hundred times over. But as Marley seemed to have something on her mind, I figured I'd tell her about my discovery later.

"You okay, Mar? You seem bothered."

"It's my readership," she admitted. "The numbers are dismal. I may go down in Triton history as *the* most unsuccessful editor *The Armada* has ever had," she complained. "And as an overachiever, I don't handle failure well."

I bent down to tighten my shoelace. "Gee, Mar. I wish there was something I could do to help."

Recess was just about over, so Marley began to put her things away in her book bag. "Thanks, Willa. If you come up with something, I'd love to hear it." Marley gave me a quick hug.

"Homos!" Somebody yelled.

But it didn't bother me in the least. I was still riding high from my afternoon with Cody.

***

Robbie sat at a lunch table all by himself. Well, he sat in his *wheelchair* that was pushed up to one of the cement tables. I sauntered up to the table to say hi. ("Sauntered" is my new word for the day. I'm working on increasing my vocabulary.)

Robbie wasn't drooling—well maybe he was, because his chin was wet, but I think it was from the juice box that he was sucking on through a straw, stuck in a cup holder on top of his tray. He bent his head down from time to time to take a sip. It must have been orange-flavored, because he looked like he'd been eating Cheetos. Cody's neon cap was pulled tight on his head.

I said hello and then reached inside my backpack for a paper towel. I'd come prepared. Oddly enough, that kind of stuff doesn't make me gag—the wiping of body fluids. A medical career might be in my future. Or dog groomer. Those people have to wipe that nauseating goo out of dogs' eyes and even sometimes press that gland in their rear ends to get out that smelly stuff. The trapped poop or something.

"How's it going?" I asked, smiling at him. "Making much headway on the tryouts for the track and field team?" I joked. Sometimes it's just best to address the elephant in the room.

"Naww, traak en feel," he said. "Poole vall," he joked back, twisting his head to the left.

"Pole vault? That's hysterical!" The kid has a sense of humor. I laughed so hard I almost wet my pants. Keiran and Brylee walked by, giving us odd looks and shaking their heads, saying something about "deserving each other."

"If you really want to impress the ladies, you need to try out for band. I'm thinking the flute."

"Naww, fluute. Guutarr."

"Guitar! Perfect. Girls love guys who can play the guitar. It's so romantic." And I put my hands together and fluttered my eyelashes the same way Lucy does to Schroeder in all the Charlie Brown movies.

Of course we were both teasing. Sadly, the chances of Robbie ever running were slim. And CP can result in degenerative arthritis and constriction of the hands, making it impossible to accomplish even the simplest of tasks, so the guitar was probably out. Not that there wasn't always reason for hope. Because, *"Once you choose hope, anything is possible."* ~ Christopher Reeve as quoted by Marley Applegate.

I continued chuckling, even going so far as slapping Robbie on the back—well, it was more of a gentle tap on his shoulder—in exchange for the good guffaw, but mostly so it gave me a chance to touch him. Not in a sicko, pervy sort of way, but in the sort of way that says to a CP kid they are just the same as you and me, and deserve to be touched.

A group of seventh graders walked by, boys and girls, and I smiled and said, "This guy is a riot!" pointing to Robbie. And because they were seventh graders, they had to take my word for it. Because I may not have been one of the cool kids, but I was at least an *older* kid—an eighth grader. Dweebie or not.

Other kids walked by, not close—heaven only knows, we might be contagious—but near enough that they could tell we were having a pretty good time together.

"So here's one for you. I'm not the best joke-teller, because I usually forget the punch line, but here goes. What time should a person go to the dentist?"

Robbie shook his shoulders. He also shook his right leg and his left arm, but the shoulder shake meant he didn't know the answer.

"At tooth thirty! Get it? TOOTH THIRTY! You know, instead of two—tooth?" I slapped myself on the leg. I'm such a riot. Although now I'll have to pay my dad a royalty, because the joke is actually his. Dentist humor and all that.

"How about you? Ya got any zingers?"

Dakota and Dallas walked by, dressed far too hoochie for a school day in their short skirts and too much makeup. Dakota barked "Losers!" and did that L thing in the middle of her forehead with her two fingers, which only brought more attention to that big red zit in the middle of it.

"Eers un," Robbie said, his body pitching slightly to the left. "Waare … duus thaaa … Eees er … Bahh nee gaw too … eeet breac … faasst?"

"I don't know. Where does the Easter Bunny go to eat breakfast?"

"Ahht … I…haawwp."

"IHOP!" I shouted. "Pure gold!" I said, loving the joke, because after all, I'm a total breakfast girl, and next to sweetened box cereal, pancakes at IHOP are my favorite things to eat. "Robbie Wise, I do believe we are going to become good friends," I said, getting ready to dash because I was going to be late again for class. I leaned in to give him a quick hug.

What can I say? He had me at IHOP.

CHAPTER 11

Death and sickness can have a way of putting your life in perspective.

I followed Marley and her mom down the long hallway of the hospital, stopping from time to time to admire the colorful pictures and drawings on the walls, all painted by the children—the up-and-coming Monets and the Rembrandts of the pediatric ward. They were colorful and cheery, except for one—a disturbing acrylic that looked a lot like *The Scream*, by Munch—or maybe the movie promo for *Home Alone,* because both the boys had their hands on their cheeks and that horrified look on their faces.

Marley's mom, Dr. Applegate, (a whimsical name for such an exotic woman!) stopped in one room or another, with Marley and me following along as a way to make her visit less official she told us, less scary for the kids, the sweet little things sick with cancer. We handed out small toys and crayons, except to the one little girl who was trapped inside a plastic bubble, the result of a severely compromised immune system, according to Marley. To her we waved and chatted, and Marley made a balloon animal with a yellow balloon she had in her front pocket. Yet another talent my friend possesses: balloon animal-maker. Who knew?

Dr. Applegate and Marley stopped to speak with a sad family all gathered around a little boy who seemed to be very sick, far sicker than the rest. Not wanting to intrude, I wandered into the room across the hall, beckoned inside by the sound of someone crying.

"Are you okay?" I asked the girl who sat up in her bed alone in her room. She was probably around my age and may once have had a head of pretty red hair, judging by the color of the remaining few on her head. She had snow-white skin tinged with green, and she was missing all of her eyebrows and eyelashes, making her look like a friendly alien.

A crying alien, but friendly, nonetheless.

"Do I *look* okay to you?" She held up her arms, attached to monitors by assorted tubes, and then she pointed to her head. The cancer hadn't affected her sense of humor.

"Umm …" I stammered, not knowing which direction to take. Going for the one that felt right, I said, "I don't know. What did you look like before? Bald for Fall, New Look, New You," I piped, picking up and holding a teen magazine that littered her bedside tray and pointing to the cover. "You might start the newest craze in your school. And may I say you have a very nicely shaped head." I may have gone a bit overboard with my last remark, but it was too soon to tell.

The girl chuckled. She probably would have laughed if she'd had the strength, which she didn't.

"What are you in for? Armed robbery? Petty theft? Indecent exposure?" I asked.

That time, she did laugh. She laughed so hard the monitors started going crazy, blinking and beeping, until a voice came on over a speaker asking if she needed help.

"I'm all right!" she assured, after pressing a button and speaking aloud and over her shoulder to no one that I could see.

"*Indecent exposure*," she repeated, smiling and blinking her big blue alien eyes at me. "You slay me." She held out the hand that was less covered in tubes than the other. "Delores Wannamaker," she said, introducing herself as we shook hands. "Non-Hodgkin's lymphoma."

"Wilhelmina Shisbey," I introduced back. "Diarrhea of the mouth. It's a pleasure to meet you."

"Yikes!" she said.

"Yikes because of the name, or yikes the disease?"

"Name. A little Kaopectate should cure the other."

"Tell me about it."

"Yeah. Yours is a rough one, but it's still not as bad as Wannamaker. 'Hey, Dolores,' she parroted, her voice going falsetto, 'you wannamaker baby with me?' or 'Dolores, wannamaker me some nachos? Extra cheese.'"

"Life sucks," I agreed.

"Totally," Dolores said. "I can't seem to remember a time when it was good."

"Never?" I took a seat in the chair next to Dolores's bed, scooting it over closer to her. Dolores didn't seem to mind. Not that I asked her permission.

"Not really," she sighed, and something must have happened because Dolores sort of moaned, and she turned her body away from me to face the wall while she tried to breathe through her pain.

And as I sat there watching Dolores, something occurred to me. It was something we were studying in Mr. Bennett's class, about laughter being contagious, how the premotor cortical part of the brain responds to the sound of it. My idea started small, but it grew, the same way a snowball gains momentum.

"Dee, let's play a game," I said.

"Soccer? Dodge ball? You pick."

I brought my legs up on the chair and sat Indian-style, smiling at Dolores. "No, it's a memory game.

See, I have this sort of weird thing with memory, in that I have a really amazing one. But instead of holding on to the good things that happen, I totally obsess over all the bad ones. I mean, the really sucky ones, like the memory of my mom giving me up for adoption when I was a baby, and the fact that I was born with a cleft and the bottom of my face was mangled. And, of course, then there're these …" I said and pointed to my glasses.

"Yeah, too bad you weren't born beautiful, like me," Dee said, playing along with me. We shared a laugh.

"Let's play *'I remember when …'* Let's each take a turn thinking about a *good* memory, any memory that made us laugh, or was crazy or silly, and see if we both can't find a spot of sunshine on a cloudy day!" It was total overkill and I knew it.

"Oh, *puh-leeze.* If I hadn't vomited right before you came in, I'd vomit again." She pointed to a plastic kidney-shaped dish covered with a napkin and resting on the nightstand beside her. I wasn't about to remove the napkin, so I had to take her word for it. "Tone down the perky. Would ya? It's *way* too early in the day for you to be psychotically cheerful."

I forgave her remarks because I knew Dolores didn't feel well. "I'll start," I said, adjusting myself on my chair. I was on a do-gooder mission, and nothing was going to stop me. "I remember the day I first tasted ice cream," I began.

"Vanilla or chocolate?"

"Strawberry. And nice try. This is about *feelings*, it's not as if there's going to be a quiz after."

"Fine. I'll play, because, obviously, you aren't going to let me get out of it. And since I'm all but tied to this bed by chains, you currently have me at a disadvantage." Dee sat up a little straighter in the bed, tapping her baldhead with her finger. "Okay, I got one. The day I got my cat, Eleanor."

"Eleanor? Odd name for a cat."

"Strange you say that, … *Wilhelmina*."

"Disneyland, Saturday, October 7, 2006. Loved, *loved* Space Mountain," I said.

"I thought you said there wasn't going to be a quiz. What's with the dates?" Dee drummed her fingers on the mattress of her hospital bed and thought for a second. "First kiss. Fifth grade—Ricky Ettinger. All lips, no tongue."

"Eww …"

And so it went, Dee and I sharing memories. All good ones—laughing and having a fun time. Some memories were as simple as how the rain felt when it touched our skin, or the smell of the flowers in spring, or the new doll that we got for Christmas the year that we were nine.

I left Dee's room after a while, when she started to tire. Marley and her mom were still in the room with the family of the little boy, waiting for something, it seemed. I wasn't sure what. And I continued my "game," going to other rooms, with parental consent, of course, if they were in there. If the kid was alone, I went in anyway and figured better to ask for forgiveness than to ask for permission. I played *I remember when* with the girls and the boys, recalling what Mr. Bennett had said about laughter being contagious, just like a yawn.

Marley finally found me in Jenny Hunter's room, a little girl with leukemia.

"It's time to go," Marley said, and I could tell

that she'd been crying. She pulled a tissue out of her dress pocket and blew her nose.

I said good-bye to Jenny and told her to hold onto the memories, as cliché as it sounds, and I followed Marley into the hallway, where her mother stood with a sad expression on her face.

"He died?" I asked. "The little boy whose room you were in. He died?" I repeated, knowing it must be true.

Dr. Applegate wiped a tear from her eye. I'm sure no matter how many times it happened, it was never easy for her, and I thought how terrible it must be to have a job where sometimes there was nothing you could do to help.

"Yes, he did," she answered sadly. She gathered Marley and me to her in a tight hug. "Thank you, girls," she whispered, kissing us each on the top of our head. She released us and then pulled up the sleeve of her lab coat and looked at her watch. "Come on, let's go. I think we all need some ice cream."

CHAPTER 12

I dipped a fry in some ketchup and stuffed it in my mouth. We were having Big Macs at McDonald's. Not at one that Cody's family owns, because they're like a city away and my dad wasn't willing to drive there.

"Dad," I said, "can I ask you a question?"

My dad held up one finger to mean he needed a second to swallow first. Dad finally swallowed, his Adam's apple increasing in size when he did and looking like a snake that has eaten a mouse. "Shoot," he finally said.

"What does 'the end justifies the means' mean?"

My dad wiped his mouth and took a sip of his Diet Coke. *Diet*—as if that helps. The calorie content on a Big Mac, according to the Basic Nutrition Facts sheet I'd snatched from the counter, is 560. Although zero calories come from alcohol, according to the info, so that's all good. It also has 1,010 mg. of sodium, and 2,343 kilojoules, whatever that is. Sounds toxic to me. No wonder Diane said she couldn't come to dinner with us. She said it would ruin her recent colonic, and Olivia didn't come because she claims she's gone vegan.

"The end justifies the means ... means," he said, chuckling at the double word use, "using bad or immoral methods as long as you accomplish something good by using them." He began to tidy his food tray and folded up his hamburger wrapper so that it resembled a mailing envelope. "Why do you ask?"

I slurped on my chocolate McCafé shake, (720 calories for a 16-ounce, versus a whopping 1,160 for the 32-ouncer had I gone with the Chocolate Triple Thick. Honestly, it's a wonder Cody and his brothers aren't 500 pounds!)

"I'm working on something for school. A project, you could say."

"I couldn't say anything of the sort." Dad winked.

"A project, *one* could say," I corrected, assuming the one was me. "Or maybe it's not so much a project as it is a 'social experiment.'" I used air quotes.

"Are you asking my permission?" Dad started wiping down the table with his napkin.

Sometimes I think that maybe my dad is my *real* father, with how much we are alike. In my dreams he's my real dad, only in my dreams he looks like Kyle Chandler, the guy who played the dad, and head football coach, Eric Taylor, on *Friday Night Lights*. The hottest of the hot dads.

"Because if you are, let me ask you two questions." Dad pulled a pre-moistened towelette from the front pocket of his slacks and cleaned his hands with it. "Will anyone be hurt by your actions—emotionally or physically—and will your actions result in making someone's life better by you doing … well, whatever it is that you're planning on doing?"

"No and yes," I answered, grabbing my tray and

heading to the trashcan. When I returned, my dad had the van keys in his hand and was ready to go.

"In that case, Willa, you have my permission."

***

My plan was genius. Pure genius. And it had to be from spending time with Marley and Cody—that their smarts were rubbing off on me. Could it be their intelligence brain molecules, or atoms, or whatever, were somehow infiltrating my brain? Seeping into it and making me smarter just by the sheer proximity of them? Smart by association? Then again, I just reread those lines aloud and realize how lame they sound. Dumb even. So, no, maybe I'm not as smart as I thought. But my plan had merit. Of that I was sure.

It was still in its infancy, my plan. Some rough edges that would have to be smoothed. And then there was the fact that it wouldn't work at all without Cody helping me with it, and who knows if he'd even want to?

I skipped along on my way to school … Omigod. I skipped! I actually caught myself skipping, but caught myself just as I saw a group of kids up ahead of me waiting for the passing guard to come and help them cross the street. I resumed my walking at a pace that might be considered more of an amble. Not only was my mood light enough that it made me want to skip, but I'd resumed my raiding of Olivia's closet, and I was wearing a light-pink button-down shirt.

Sure, for Olivia it was actually a costume—the shirt she wore when she was in a production of *Grease* back at her middle school in Lincoln Park. She played one of the pink ladies, which meant I had to tear off the big P that was sewn on the front of it. But the color suited me and it went okay with my old jeans and my sneakers … I mean "tennis" shoes.

I keep forgetting that in California kids don't call them sneakers. I don't know why. They look nothing like the shoes Diane wears to play tennis and in the entire time I've been in California, I've never once seen a kid play tennis. Actually, I've never once even heard a kid mention the word tennis in reference to the sport, only the shoe.

I was walking/skipping/ambling to school by myself because Marley went to school early to do something with the paper. It seems that Omar thought the readership might improve if the photos were all in color. He thought the picture of the dead beached whale in the environmental section of the paper would have had more impact if the kids could see its blood, and that the shot of the cheeseburger crawling with maggots in the "foods" section (FYI: the burger was in the trash, it's not like it was being served as the daily lunch special), would have had a more "visceral effect," (his words, not mine) on the students. But Marley wasn't convinced, so she went in early to make sure he didn't go forward with his plan.

The first group of kids had already crossed at the crosswalk, escorted like ducklings following their mother—if their mother was an old bearded man carrying a big red stop sign and wearing a yellow-and-orange vest covered with reflective tape. A second group waited for their turn. Cody and Conner were part of that group, but thankfully the evildoer twins were missing.

"Hi, Cody. Hey, Connor. How's Dude?" I said.

"He's good," Connor answered, and I noticed for the first time that Connor had a bit of a lisp. It sounded like he'd said, "heath good." "Everybody liketh hith YouTube video," he said, shyly, dropping his gaze to stare at the cracks in the sidewalk.

"Totally," Cody interjected. "The thing has more than fifty thousand hits so far. Now, if we could only figure out a way to monetize it, we might just make us some money." Cody zipped the zipper of his gray sweatshirt up and down as if he were strumming a guitar.

"Cool," I said, trying to sound cool by saying the word "cool." The light changed and we all followed the guard across the street, the elementary kids going one way and the middle-schoolers another. Cody said good-bye to his brother.

"Can I talk to you for a second, Cody?" I asked.

"A second?" Cody asked, chuckling, turning his black Volcom hat so the brim was in the back. He smiled at me and whatever it is I wanted to discuss with him flew right out of my brain as I stared at his lips. His eyes. His nose. His dimple …

"Chicago," Cody said, bringing me back to the present. "When have you *ever* only taken a 'second' to talk?"

He had me there. I asked him to at least give me to the front entrance of school. Cody nodded and started walking with me.

"I need a favor from you, Cody."

"Sorry, Chicago. This body's not for sale," he joked, unzipping his jacket to reveal his chest (covered by a long-sleeved Quicksilver tee).

"Not even for a million?" I joked back.

"Dollars or clams? If it were dollars, I'd consider it." He dimpled again. "What do you need, Chicago?" he asked, more seriously.

Cody was still tutoring me and now my dad was actually paying him—once my grades in math started going up and my dad figured it wasn't all just some ruse I was using to get a popular boy to come to my house.

I considered Cody to be my friend and I think he felt the same way about me. It's not as if we sat together at the same table at lunch or anything, talking and hanging out. Cody's table had invisible Do Not Cross tape stretched around the perimeter of it, the same way a CSI crime scene does. If you weren't one of the cool kids—the popular, the awesome, or the glam—you weren't crossing that line.

"Okay, so this may sound totally stupid, but give me a minute to explain my plan."

"Your plan?" Cody sounded intrigued.

"Yeah, my plan. It's a way to make people accept Robbie—he's the new kid," I added, in case Cody had forgotten. "And maybe help Marley out with the lack of interest in the school paper."

"I'm all ears," Cody said.

As far as I'm concerned, Cody was much more than ears. The ears were just one more adorable part.

"You've heard of the story *The Emperor's New Clothes*, right?"

"The story of the naked dude?"

"That would be the one."

"There you go again, Chicago. It's all about the bod. What? You want to see me—"

"No!" I blurted out. Omigod, this conversation was seriously taking a wrong turn. "No," I insisted, "just hold on and let me explain." I hitched my pack higher on my shoulder. "I want to try something, Cody, and I need your power."

"My power?" Cody asked, his forehead wrinkling.

"The story of *The Emperor's New Clothes*—and I'm sure you know this because you are really smart and just dumbing it down, for some reason known only to you—is about something called pluralistic ignorance."

"Pluralistic ignorance," Cody repeated. "A bias *about* a social group, held *by* a social group," Cody said, either knowing it or pulling it out of his ... Out of thin air.

"Exactly!" I exclaimed, impressed Cody knew the definition. "The theory explains how people are more likely to help in an emergency when alone than if others are near, but if one lends a hand, then the others will follow."

"I get that, but what does this have to do with me and my 'power,' as you call it?" We had arrived at Triton's ivy-covered brick walls, the dolphin smiling at us from his tiled position embedded into the bricks.

"Your power, Cody Cassidy, and your mission should you be willing to accept it, is the power of popularity. I want you to pretend that Robbie Wise, the new kid in school in the wheelchair, is the funniest joke-teller you have ever heard. The best knee-slapping, eye-watering, pants-peeing, funniest guy *ever*—short of Carrot Top, maybe, who personally I can't stand, but others seem to enjoy."

Cody stopped walking and he scratched his head. "*Chicago* ..." he drew out, so that it sounded more like a sigh. "The guy barely *talks*. How can I make people believe he's funny if he doesn't even talk?" He shook his head. "I don't know. It sounds farfetched to me."

"But he does talk! He talks up a storm. And he's funny! Honest to goodness, Cody, I'm not making this up. Robbie is really funny. He tells the greatest jokes. He's got a million of them. He cracks me up every day."

"I just don't think it will work, Chicago. If no

one can understand the guy but you, it just won't work." Cody shook his head.

I clenched my hands and held them by my sides in frustration. "But they *will*, Cody! That's part of my plan. The kids *will* understand him. Just wait. I'm working on something right now as we speak. Trust me. Please," I begged. "This will work. I know it will. *Please* say you'll help me." I reached out and tugged the sleeve of his jacket.

Cody stared at me as the tears of passion for my plan brightened my eyes and my face flushed red. Cody pulled off his hat and replaced it, brim forward, and the light of kindness that shined in his eyes made him even more handsome.

"All right, Chicago. I'll help," he said, reaching out and casually draping his arm around my shoulder for just a moment as we entered the campus. "I'll use this supposed *power* of mine for good. Just let me know what you want me to do."

***

I approached Robbie where he sat underneath a sycamore tree planted just outside the quad. It was recess and Marley was under the gun with her deadlines for the paper, so I decided to spend some time with a friend who looked as if he could use one. I don't know why kids are so freaked out by a little drool and an occasional twitch.

We fist bumped hello. "Robbie, how come you don't have a communication device? One of those voice synthesizers like Stephen Hawking. Then everyone would know how smart and funny you are."

Robbie's head did an involuntary counter-clockwise motion. At least I think it was involuntary. "Naoo … mawn … keey," he said.

"No monkey?" Robbie nodded his head left to right. I couldn't tell if that meant he was affirming that no, he did not have a monkey, or that my guess of "no monkey" was incorrect.

"Tooo …spen …siivve," he said, landing me back to square one, because I bet monkeys are super expensive and that's why only zoos can afford them. Robbie pointed to his knee with his left hand. "Nee … mawn nee."

"Money! I get it now. Duh!" Yes, money made total sense. Monkey, not so much.

Cody approached with Jax and Dylan, and they walked right by us. Cody winked at me as he passed and then he turned around, and he double-backed over. Without any reason to do so, Cody let loose a huge howl of laughter, roaring and holding his stomach as if he needed to hold himself in one piece. Snorting and guffawing and totally going overboard.

"Hysterical, dude!" he practically shouted, while raising his shoulders up and down, in a poor performance of someone laughing. "You're a riot! A total riot!" Cody laughed his fool head off.

"Cody!" I hissed. "We haven't started the plan yet. Robbie didn't even *say* anything! For goodness' sake, Cody, *stop*. Kids are staring."

Cody was making a scene. Kids were turning toward us, but instead of looks of pity or disgust on their faces—the expressions they usually had when they passed Robbie—they showed interest. Even without the plan in place, Cody's theatrics may actually have been working. Unfortunately, they worked so well, it also attracted his girlfriend.

"Cody! Babe, what on *earth* are you doing?"

Dakota asked him, looking horrified and going to stand next to him while her sister flanked him on the other side, penning Cody in the middle—the creamy center filling of Dakota's Oreo cookie.

I rolled my eyes and wanted to gag at the "babe," which I'm sure she said solely for my benefit.

Ever since Dakota found out Cody had been in my bedroom, the day of the disastrous sleepover party at my house, Dakota's had him on a short leash and has turned up the volume on the cutesy names. Besides babe, I've also heard her call Cody sweetheart, darlin', sugar, and my personal biggest, all-time, make-me-puke favorite—*pookie bear.* But cutesy names or not, Cody's says he's now spent more time at my house than he has at Dakota's. So, guess what Dakota? I win!

"Come on, Cody," Dakota said and turned around and pulled Cody by the hood of his sweatshirt, using it like a leash and snapping his head back with the force of it. "You're going to catch their cooties," she said, using a word that is so old-fashioned it was taken out of circulation somewhere around the time my dad went to middle school. If Dakota had any smarts at all, she would know that the term *cooties* refers to head lice, something, Marley told me in confidence, Dakota had a bad case of in third grade.

As the story goes, the school nurse sent Dakota home so her mom could delouse her and when she returned to school, Dakota was wearing a shirt that said, "Head lice doesn't discriminate," in a way that meant she was somehow the victim of a crime.

"Oww, Dakota!" Cody said, "Quit pulling on me." She let go. Cody straightened, and he tipped his chin at me before heading off with the two girls.

Later, in math class, (where I got a B on my pop quiz and Cody got an intentional D for some reason, his paper nearly empty of answers I know he knew, but looking pretty awesome with his doodles of pictures of Dude riding a surfboard and tubed by a wave), Cody leaned toward me from his desk behind me, and he said, "Nice plan."

I couldn't turn around because Mrs. Deejet, ("Numbers are my name!" she likes to say. Deejet-*Digit*) was looking my way, so I wrote a note and passed it back to him that said, "You rock! Only next time, wait for the punch line."

"Wilhelmina! Is there something you'd like to share with the class?" Mrs. Deejet said in her Indian accent. That's East Indian, not Native American. Do Native Americans even have an accent?

"No, thank you, Mrs. Deejet," I answered.

The class giggled and Dustin, who sits in the back so the teachers don't see him constantly texting, said "Busted." And I don't know if Mrs. Deejet's question was rhetorical, but there's no way I was disclosing my plan to her—or the class.

I heard Cody's pencil scratching on a piece of paper. A second later he tapped me on the back with the tip of his eraser and he handed me a note. The paper was folded in a small triangle, the way all the boys fold paper in the shapes of a tortilla chip, so they can play that football game thing with it and flick it through imaginary goalposts with their fingers. I opened it and it read, *Sorry. I'll do better next time.*

"Wilhelmina!" Mrs. Deejet snapped. And it must have been her time of the month because she stormed down the aisle and grabbed the note right out of my hand. Then she walked back up to the board, and she stood there and read the note aloud. And the way she read it, it came out all suggestively, or maybe it was the accent, but it sounded *so* wrong. Of course, all the kids just *loved* that Cody Cassidy was telling the nerdy girl that he was going to "do better next time." And I knew that before first lunch, Dakota was going to hear about it and that I'd better start sleeping with one eye open.

CHAPTER 13

"*I hate him!*" Olivia screamed dramatically, racing through the front door, her hair as wild as Medusa's (but minus the snakes) and her black mascara running down her face in muddy streams. She saw me standing there on my way to the bathroom and she turned on me, the rabid dog that she is. "And I *hate* you, too!"

"Me?" I squeaked. "What did I do?" Not that for Olivia there ever needed to be a valid reason. In the past, I've had Olivia hate me because: it was raining outside, she broke a fingernail, she gained two pounds, she misplaced her favorite lipstick, and once because the zipper got stuck on her cheerleading skirt and she had to use a safety pin to keep it closed.

I scrunched up my face to stare at her. (My glasses were off, and usually when they are I do weird stuff with my eyes.)

"Denver broke up with me! He broke up with *me!*" she said, pointing to herself with one of her talons, as if there might have been some confusion. Olivia tore off her metallic pink scarf and flung it across the room, where it landed only twelve inches away from her. "And it's all your fault! I wish you'd never been born!"

I wish you'd never been born …

Harsh. And not the first time Olivia's ever said it. When I was younger, I used to respond with *I'm water and you're glue. Whatever you say bounces off me and sticks to you!* But now that I'm older, I realize how stupid that saying is.

I wish you'd never been born … I wonder if my birth mom said the same thing when she first looked at me.

I can't really find fault with Olivia for saying those words, because it's something that I've said myself many times. Only mine was, "I wish *I* was never born." A line that almost every kid alive has probably said because they weren't allowed to go to the movies or their mom served them liver for dinner, clueless as to how much life can really suck. The bigger question here was why I'd somehow been lumped in with Denver, although I planned to find out.

"Olivia?" I knocked on the door to Olivia's room. I would have walked in, but I tried the knob and it was locked.

"Go away!"

Reaching into my pocket, I pulled out a hairpin and used it to open the door.

"*I said go away!*" she screamed, completely unhinged. "Mom!" she yelled.

"Mom's not home. She left a note saying there was a last-minute cancellation at Eyefull and she went to get eyelash extensions." I went over to Olivia's desk chair and took a seat.

"*I—said—get—out!*"

"Is that what you *really* want, Olivia?" I asked calmly and maintaining eye contact. "Let's discuss how you feel right now and what events may have led up to your latest relapse. What would you say your trigger points are?" I'd been watching *Celebrity Rehab With Dr. Drew*, so I knew all the lingo. Olivia looked at me as if I'd gone totally bonkers.

"What are you talking about?"

"I'm here to *help*, Olivia," I said. "Why won't you let me?" And I gave this huge sigh in a Dr. Drew way that indicated helping addicts was sometimes just more than I could stand.

"Get away from me, you freak!" Olivia scooted up on her bed so that she was crouched against the headboard, her legs tight against her body in an effort to escape me. "Daaad!"

I dropped the act. "Dad's not home. His car's in the driveway because he went with Mom to the eyelash place. Not to get eyelashes, but because it's next to Whole Foods and there are some exotic cheeses they just got in that he wants to check out."

I advanced on Olivia. Having Cody as my friend was giving me confidence I'd never had before. And if I may be so vulgar as to say, I just think I may have grown me a set of ... *gonads*.

"So, tell me, *dear sister*," I continued, "what have

I supposedly done now?" I gave Olivia the "Willa Stare." Basically, it's stink eye with less stink and more attitude. I'm still trying to perfect it.

"Why are your eyes crossed? Eww, gross, you nerd, I think you need to put on your glasses."

Olivia was right; my eyes were definitely feeling some eyestrain. I left the room and then came back with my glasses on. "So, what's your problem? Besides me?" And I said it with a nice voice that brought on more tears from Olivia.

"Denver went out with that skanky Lowenstein chick with the big boobs while I was grounded. Rumor has it, she's … well, you know … *fast*. And I'm not talking track and field."

"*Yikes*! I'm sorry." Not that it was my fault, because it wasn't. It's not as if I can control the girl's overgrown mammaries or the fact she has the morals of a genus Rattus—that's roof rat to you and me.

"Plus, Denver said that he could no longer take my midwestern accent. I don't have a midwestern accent. *You* may have one, but I sure don't," she said. "*Do I?*" she asked tearfully.

For a minute, I really did feel sorry for her. But then I remembered March 9th, seven years ago, the time Olivia locked me out of the house during a snowstorm when I was only six, and my sympathy for her quickly passed. (The rest of the story is that my dad soon drove up and let me in and gave me a hot bath and made me hot chocolate, so it had a happy ending.)

I wandered over to Olivia's dresser and started messing with her stuff right in front of her. "Yeah, Olivia, you sorta have an accent. But look at the bright side, we could have come from North Dakota, and then you'd be going around saying things like *"The odds are ahundderd to one da Vikin's will win da Super Bowl— don-chya-no?"* I said, imitating the people from that movie *Fargo*. I picked up her comb from the dresser and drew my thumb across the plastic teeth, liking the sound it made, *zzzrrrwwwffttt*. "But come on, he's a total loser if he dumped you because he doesn't like your accent."

"You think so?" Olivia's blue eyes went wide.

"I know so."

If Denver dumped Olivia because she was a shallow, self-centered, egomaniacal, petty sociopath, I would say he's an astute observer of the darker side of human nature, but as it was solely on account of her accent, he was a total loser.

Since Olivia and I were making some major progress, I went so far as to sit on the end of her bed. She didn't slug me, which was a good thing. "Now tell me some of the other reasons why you hate me." It felt good to finally have a chance to clear the air with her. Maybe I needed to watch Dr. Drew more often. A career in psychology might be in the stars for me.

"Where do I start? There are *so* many reasons why I hate you."

"Let's just start with one."

"If I start, I may not be able to stop."

"Que sera sera," I said philosophically.

"Since when did you start speaking Chinese?"

"It's not Chinese, it's … forget it."

Olivia picked at her cuticle. "I don't have a good memory like you. So, I'll start with the most recent reasons why I hate you and work back if I can still remember them."

"Fire away."

"There's the grounding," Olivia said, using her first finger.

"We covered that one. Let's keep moving forward. It's important in therapy not to dwell." I took off my glasses and wiped at a smudge with the bottom of my shirt.

"Then there's the issue that you somehow keep managing to tick off Dakota and then I have to hear all about it from Denver. That you're a weaselly *boyfriend stealer.* Not that I believe for a single second that a hot boy like Cody would *ever* like you when he can have Dakota or Dallas, or both of 'em, if he were smart."

"I don't see Cody as the kind of guy who would do something like that," I said, defending him.

"Who cares!" Olivia flung herself dramatically across the bed, her body facing down on her comforter, her pretty blonde head just inches away from me. "It's over! Denver and I are over." Her shoulders heaved and real tears flowed from her eyes.

And right then, I felt genuinely sorry for Olivia, as strange as it sounds, as Olivia cried, her mascara ruining her expensive duvet.

"Don't cry, Olivia." I awkwardly patted her shoulder. "Look at all the good in your life. How pretty you are, how popular. You're so lucky."

Olivia raised her tear-streaked face to me. "Lucky? Willa. *I'm lucky?* What about love? Love! That's what I want. I want Denver to love me ... and Mom and Dad."

"Mom and Dad love you," I volunteered, hoping the word "Mom" sounded more normal than it felt to say it.

Olivia snorted, and a little snot bubble came out. "Mom only loves herself," she moaned, on the verge of crying again. "Do you know that not *once* has she come to one of the football games to watch me cheer? Not once! She says that the games are the same time as her Zumba class. Zumba is more important to Mom than her own daughter. And what the heck is Zumba anyway?"

"It's an exercise class that combines high energy and loud Latin music in order to allow participants to dance away their worries," I rattled off, sounding like I was a paid spokesperson for the feel-happy workout promising to burn 500-800 calories a session.

I thought about what Olivia said for a second. I knew that Diane didn't love *me*. But I was pretty sure she loved Olivia, the "fruit of her loins."

"What about Dad? He loves you," I said, silently agreeing that Olivia's view of her mother was correct. I don't even think Diane was that into Dad, although she seems to like him more now that he took her out of that "one stoplight town," as she called our Chicago suburb.

Olivia got up from the bed and went to her mirrored closet doors to fix her makeup, wiping underneath her eyes to remove the mascara with her finger and opening her mouth while she did it. (Why do women do that? Note to self: must investigate.)

Olivia got most of the mascara, but her eyes still glistened with tears. "Dad loves me, but he loves you more," she accused. "*Way* more."

"He does not," I said, but a small part of me hoped that it was true, and an even smaller part—a teeny tiny part … knew that it might be true. My dad and I are kindred spirits, one could say.

"Does so!" she shot back. Olivia continued to stand in front of the mirror, talking to me via her reflection in the glass. "He *chose* you, Willa! Dad chose you because he loves you! He saw you in that orphanage, all homely and messed up, and it was all he could talk about. That 'special little girl,' he'd call you, 'the girl with the abominable spirit.'"

"I'm pretty sure the word you're looking for is *indomitable*. It means courageous. Abominable is like … the scary snowman. The Yeti," I corrected her.

"*Whatever!* All I know is that Dad would come home from that orphanage after fixing those kids' teeth, yammering on about this one kid, Willa. How great you were, what an inspiration to other kids, and how helpful … blabbing on about you so much that Mom and I were sick of hearing him."

Olivia was crying again, big sobs that made her chest heave and her face swell as the tears continued to fall.

"He chose you, Willa! Just the same way as I chose those cute strappy sandals because I loved them and just *had* to have them." Olivia pointed to some new shoes in a box on the floor, and they were adorable, I have to say. "But not me," Olivia continued. "Me? I'm like the crummy presents from Nana Davis at Christmas; the goofy pajamas or the scented body talc you're forced to accept because it's a gift. The present you didn't want, but aren't allowed to throw away, because after all, you got it as a stupid gift."

"Come on, Olivia, you know that's not true."

"I'm the unasked-for gift, Willa! That's what I am! And you, Willa, you're the cute strappy sandals Dad couldn't live without!"

I sat shocked. Shocked in a good way — a glorious way — a way that warmed me from my head to my toes and back up again. I'd never heard Olivia say these things and I would never have even allowed myself to think them, but I knew she was right. My dad *had* chosen me. Above all those other kids my dad saw over the years, dozens and dozens of them, possibly even hundreds. My dad chose me, maybe even above Olivia, his natural child, the *you-get-what-you-get* kid, like a surprise grab bag at the dollar store that's usually filled with the leftover crud that no one wants to buy.

Above all those other kids my dad saw over the years—and maybe even over his own natural daughter—my dad chose me.

CHAPTER 14

W as it me, or was my cereal sweeter, my sun sunnier, and my deodorant more absorbent? It was a glorious day. For the first time I could ever remember, Olivia let me borrow her clothes. She actually *invited* me into her room and let me choose a top to wear to school. So sure, it had to be from the left side of her closet, the side where the uglier stuff was, the things that needed to be repaired, or were stained and she just hadn't yet gotten around to throwing out, but still, *Olivia let me borrow her clothes!*

I'd chosen a royal blue-and-aqua striped sweater that came from Forever 21. Disappointingly, it was a little too big across the chest (no surprise there), kinda itchy, and the bottom was stretched out so that it hung lopsided on me, plus, I'd seen one just like it in the boys' section at Walmart, but still, Olivia had actually invited me into her room and let me pick it out of her closet! I paired the shirt with my old jeans. (Olivia said that sharing pants was gross, because of how my ... *you know* ... would have been too close to where her ... *you know* ... had been, and just the thought of it freaked her out.) On my feet, I wore my usual non-tennis tennis shoes.

My dad came into the kitchen just as I was gathering up my things for school. I smiled at him, my heart warm. After what Olivia had told me, I felt an even stronger connection; I loved him even more, because as Olivia said, I was my dad's strappy sandal.

"Where's Mom?" I asked him, the word coming out easier because of my good mood. "I wanted to say good-bye to her."

"Bootylicious," he said, slicing a grapefruit.

"*Excuse me?*"

"Bootylicious, it's the name of that exercise boot camp she's taking at the park. She's determined to fight Mother Nature—and win." Dad shook his head.

"How's that going for her?" I had to ask, because it was so seldom that Diane shared much with me, other than the bare minimum, and the few times she's ever asked me about *my* life she doesn't hang around long enough to listen to the answers.

My dad shrugged his shoulders as if he didn't care. Or didn't know. Or didn't care to know, about Diane's struggle with Mother Nature. As far as Dad was concerned, he liked how she looked *before* she started to do all the Orange County plastic stuff to her face and lips. When she was still recognizable as an individual, instead of looking like every other bottle blond at South Coast Plaza, a fancy mall boasting "the ultimate luxury shopping experience."

"Oh, but she did tell me to give you this message. Some woman called at 6:00 this morning for you. Mom told her you were still sleeping and the woman said not to wake you."

My dad handed me the phone message pad we keep by the landline in the kitchen.

Petra called, the note read in Diane's neat cursive.

She said to tell you "Ja" (Diane's quotes) *and "Viel gluck"* (Diane's quotes again). And, then, in parentheses—*whatever that means.*

"Woo-hoo!" I shouted, waving the message in the air while my dad smiled at me, happy that I was happy.

I kissed my dad good-bye, grabbed my backpack, and headed out the front door smiling ear to ear.

***

Marley and I walked to school together and I was so excited that I grabbed Marley's hand, and we held hands for like a minute swinging them together while we walked and talked. Until someone in a group of kids on the other side of the street yelled out, *"Two little lovebirds sittin' in a tree ..."* I knew what they were getting at and I immediately let go of Marley's hand.

My plan was all coming together, I told Marley. It was genius. I was going to get kids to see Robbie in a different light and maybe even gain him some friends; plus, I was going to save the school paper. It was all so *Afterschool Special*, or maybe one of those middle-grade books that are all the rage, about the nerdy do-gooder girls, that in the end get the hot boy, after saving Jimmy from the well and rescuing the dolphin/whale/dog/ducklings/old lady shut-in who everyone thinks is a witch.

"Wow, Willa! I'm so proud of you. You really are Spider-girl!" Marley said, her dreadlock pigtails bobbing, the curly ribbons at the bottom spirals of different colors. Marley wore a bright floral top and a pink, flouncy tutu-looking skirt over her orange leggings. For shoes, she wore black ballet flats that I'd never seen her wear before.

"And Cody's totally in on it?"

"Totally. And it's working, Marley, that's the thing. It really is working, just like *The Emperor's New Clothes*. If Cody sees it, the other kids say they see it. If Cody laughs at Robbie's jokes, everyone else laughs at them, whether they understand him or not. I know we're on shaky ground, at least until Robbie's speech synthesizer arrives, but I'm getting close. I'm getting so close, Marley, that I can almost taste it," I said, using my dad's expression, even though it may not have fit the subject.

We arrived at the front of the school and I was

so excited about all that had happened and was continuing to happen, that I went up to the dolphin embedded in the smooth tiles inside the red bricks, and I said, "I name you Daniel." And blame it on the sun or the wind, or the excitement of the day, I kissed Daniel on his shiny snout.

"*Omigod!*" Dakota screamed, coming up from goodness knows where — I swear she's a shapeshifter — and causing the blood to drain from my face. "Willa is frenching Ray! Look everybody, Willa is kissing Ray!"

"Ray?" I turned to Marley, who didn't seem bothered at all that I kissed the snout of a porcelain dolphin stuck to the side of a wall.

"His name is Ray," Marley admitted. "Someone named him that when the school was first built, don't ask me why. But hey, who knows? Daniel may be his middle name."

I was totally embarrassed. So embarrassed that I wished the ground would open up and swallow me whole, or that I could magically disappear. Dematerialize like the characters on *Star Trek*, when they enter the transporter and are converted into an energy pattern and then reconverted back into matter on a whole other planet.

The first bell rang and I ran for the entrance of school while Dakota's shouts of "Yeah, run, Willa—you dolphin frencher!" receded in the background.

The first half of the day dragged by while I waited for lunch. I sat in front of Cody at math, who got a D on his test, and yet seemed excited about it, waving it in the air and declaring, "D is for delightful!" while I thought D was also for dunce and demented, and that anyone who was intentionally getting Ds on tests needed their head examined, but grateful that with his help I managed an A-.

When the bell rang for lunch, I raced out to the lunch area to find Robbie. He was easy to spot, seated in his usual place beside the table, but now the table wasn't empty. Sitting with Robbie was Peter, a boy our P.E. teacher refers to as "spatially challenged." Peter is considerably overweight—a hundred pounds by his own admission, and so he's pretty much of a loner because of all the teasing he gets.

It gave me a good feeling to see that Robbie found a friend and if things went well, I might get into this whole philanthropic thing, and Peter might just be the next person I'd choose to benefit from all the good I was doing.

"Rob-O!" I said, bumping fists.

"Wil ... aaa!" he said back, his leg doing a little jerky thing.

Let me fill you in on a little secret. Fist bumps are a great alternative to handshaking if a person has CP. Often their hands are curled anyway, so it's much easier for them to bump than to struggle with a handshake. A nice hug is always good, too. Not that they can always hug you back, but everyone loves a good hug.

"Lay a good one on me," I said to Robbie, earning me the strangest look from Peter, who choked on his fried chicken nugget before washing it down with something that said, "protein drink," but looked suspiciously like a chocolate shake.

I signaled to Cody, who sat across the lunch area. Okay, so maybe it wasn't so much a signal as it was me waving my arms and jumping up and down while saying, "Yoo-hoo, Cody!" Dakota tried to grab him by the back of his thermal as he got up to come on over, but Cody was too quick for her.

"Hey, Chicago. Robbie," Cody said when he arrived, giving us the chin-lifting "what's up" motion. "Still rockin' the hat, I see." Cody pointed to his own, a black one, and then to Robbie.

And Robbie *was* still rockin' the hat, although not half as much as Cody was his. Robbie had been rockin' it every single day since the first day Cody had given him that hat, bright orange as a safety cone, although I'm pretty sure it had been washed since Cody first gave it to him.

Cody leaned forward to me and said quietly, "I need to talk to you, Chicago." And by the way he said it, I knew it wasn't something I'd like hearing.

"No one's stopping you," I said, and it came out sounding sharper than I'd intended. Robbie was strangely quiet, so it was almost as if he wasn't there, and Peter was too into his lunch to pay much attention to us.

"I can't tutor you this week," Cody began, and he dropped his eyes, staring at the ground. "I ... uh

…" He kicked an empty juice box with his foot. "I'm going to the mall with Dakota so she can get her dress for the school dance. She says it's important I see what she's wearing so we don't clash."

I knew why Cody was embarrassed. He was embarrassed because he knew that I didn't have a date for the dance. Who'd want to take me? The new nerd in town. The girl with the memory for the unimportant and a passion for sweetened breakfast cereal.

"No problem. In fact, if you never want to tutor me again, I understand," I said, not really meaning it. My hours with Cody studying math had been the best hours of my sad, short life. Pretending that Cody's words were no biggie, I turned to Robbie and said, "Let's hear what ya got today." I hoped my voice didn't sound as if I were about to cry. I blinked my eyes twice to dispel the tears.

Robbie slowly began, "Whaa … shoood … ahhh … shoort … syytid …" Robbie grimaced, in pain maybe, and his shoulder gave a twitch to the left before he continued, "ghhoosst … aavve?"

Cody and Peter turned to me so I could translate. "I don't know," I said. "What should a shortsighted ghost have?"

With silent steps that proves she's one of the un-dead and travels on corpse feet, Dakota appeared and she was wet-cat ticked off at me for disrupting her lunch by summoning her boyfriend.

"So. *What*, Willa?" Dakota barked at me, her nose turned up in the air, a look of disgust on her perfect face and pulling her pink alligator leather designer purse closer to her. "You speak spaz? Is that how you know what Robbie is saying? Because you speak spaz?" Some of the kids laughed and the look on Dakota's face turned to one of triumph. Dallas, who arrived just a few beats behind her sister, mirrored her look of disgust.

After what Cody had told me—how he had to cancel our session in order to go shopping with Dakota for her dress for the dance, a dance that I'd forgotten about because I was so wrapped up in my own thing, I was so angry I couldn't see straight.

Dakota's words were a reality check. The cool and the uncool would never meet. No matter how much I thought that Cody was my friend, he was nothing more than an acquaintance. A school classmate. A kid who felt pity for the homely girl from Chicago, the one with all the problems.

"God, you are *such* a dork!" Dakota said, and Dallas nodded in agreement.

I felt my stomach start to churn and there was a ringing in my ears as I glared at Dakota and her sister. But most of all, I felt an overwhelming urge to rip that smug look off both those stupid Duncan faces. What did they know about hardship, with their money and their makeup? Or exclusion? What it's like not to have any friends—kids to laugh and hang out with. Even in the womb Dakota and Dallas had someone there for them. But not me. And not Robbie. Or any of the other kids who don't fit the mold of what normal is.

I'd had it with Dakota ruining my life. I wasn't going to let her belittle or demean me ever again. My fists balled at my sides and my chest heaved, and I yelled back at her, "You know what? Yeah, Dakota. Actually, I do speak spaz! I also speak blind, deaf, gay, black, and every other language of inclusion and compassion. I'm a regular linguist of all the *loser* languages. You say I'm a dork? Well I'd rather be a dork and know that I stand for something than to be trapped inside a body poisoned by hate."

I was so hurt and angry that tears were streaming down my cheeks as I shouted at Dakota. Students left their lunch tables to come over and see what all the noise was about. Marley had arrived and she held firm to the handles of Robbie's wheelchair, where Robbie sat silent and still. Peter's eyes were wide in fear and his mouth was open, his lips covered in a milk-moustache.

Dakota stepped over to Cody, her eyes locked with mine. Possessively, she took his hand—and Cody let her—his fingers automatically interlocking with hers. Watching their solidarity was more than I could stand. And I turned and ran, blinded by my tears, pushing the gawkers out of my way without an apology.

"Chicago—wait up! Chicago, please stop!" Cody's voice rang out after me.

"Cody Cassidy! So help me ..." Dakota shrieked.

But by then I'd crossed the quad and sprinted down the stairs, past the math building, and to the gym. Throwing open the door, I ran to the girls' locker room, thankful it was vacant, and I leaned against the metal lockers, holding onto my stomach with both my hands while hot tears dripped on Olivia's blue shirt.

The double doors opened and Cody walked over, a sheepish smile spread across his face.

"So, this is what the girls' locker room looks like." Cody's eyes traveled the length of the room. "Just like the guys'," he remarked, "with the exception of that," he said, pointing to a bra hanging out of the bottom of a closed locker. "We don't have many of those lying around ours. Plus, yours smells a lot better. Ours smells like BO and wet socks."

I straightened and wiped my face with the back of my sleeve. "You're not supposed to be in here."

What on earth was Cody thinking? Coming into the girls' locker room, for goodness' sake.

"I'll take my chances." Cody came toward me and he stood in front of me, placing his arms on either side of me, shoulder height, his palms flat against the locker and trapping me against the cold metal door.

"What do you want, Cody? Why don't you go back to your girlfriend and just leave me alone?" My voice cracked.

But Cody stayed put, his face inches from mine. His black beanie swooped his hair to the side, and I noticed that despite all the time Cody spent in the ocean, his hair was really healthy and shiny, even on the ends.

"Is that what you want, Chicago? For me to leave you alone?" He was so close I could smell cinnamon on his breath. It must have been his gum. "Because I don't think you do."

"My name is *Willa*, Cody! Willa," I said, wanting Cody to finally see me for who I was. A normal thirteen-year-old girl, just like any other. "And I'm from Lincoln Park."

My eyes refilled with tears. Why was Cody doing this to me? Just whose side was he on? I thought he was my friend. Whatever game he was playing, I didn't understand the rules.

"Okay, Willa," he softly said. Coming from Cody, it sounded like a sonnet.

"You can't have it both ways! I can't be your friend if you're with Dakota. Sit or stand, but don't wobble. You've got to pick a side."

My glasses fogged and I could hardly see. Cody noticed, and he gently reached out and took them off my face, pushing my hair out of my eyes before placing them on top of my head. When he was done, he put his palms back where they were. Cody had something to say and wasn't going to let me escape until he was through.

"Why, Willa? Why do I have to pick a side? Why can't I have you as my buddy, and Dakota as my girlfriend?" His eyes never left mine.

I wanted to scream out my frustration with him, but his closeness was doing some funny things to my insides, and my mind was a jumble.

"Because, Cody—Dakota and I are polar opposites! I hate everything about Dakota and the feeling is mutual. Are you Democrat or Republican? Vanilla or chocolate? Do you want to stand up and be a voice for those who don't have one, or sit with the idiots who bully people different from them?"

Someone with popularity needed to take a stand for the kids on the outside of the circle. Someone with the power to make a difference. It wasn't going to work if it was just me. And if not Cody, then who?

Cody angrily slapped the front of the locker and I jumped. He shook his head in apology and dropped his hands, stepping back from me. He swung a leg over and straddled the bench in front of the lockers, patting the space in front of him in an invitation for me to join him. I did, and I sat facing him, not seeing him clearly, because my glasses were still on top of my head like a headband. But it didn't matter. I'd stared at Cody long and often enough; I had his face committed to memory.

Cody traced a vein on my hand with his finger. His touch made my heart pound faster and my gut do somersaults.

"Can't I be an Independent and vote depending on the issues?" He scratched the back of his neck. "Or like vanilla with chocolate swirls—or visa versa? You *know* me, Willa. You know which side I stand on." His voice had softened and he sounded sad. Looking down, he began picking at a sliver of wood on the bench. "Can I tell you a secret?" He brought his head back up to look at me, pulling off his beanie and holding it in his hands. He had hat-hair, but on Cody, even hat-hair looks good.

The five-minute bell sounded and I knew that soon the second lunch students would be coming in from the field.

"Sure. I'm all ears," I said, repeating something Cody had once said to me and immediately wishing I hadn't, because I *hate* my big ears.

"My older brother is gay," he said softly. "He came out to my father last week, although I'd guessed it for years. You may have, too. When you met him?" I shook my head no. Carter seemed just like a regular surfer guy to me. Just a regular guy who taught his dog how to surf and to ride a skateboard. "Carter said that he could no longer live the lie. That he wouldn't choose it—to be gay—if he had the choice, but that's the way he was made, and now he needs to be true to himself." Cody straightened his back and held my gaze. "When Carter told my dad, my father hit him, Willa, saying that no son of his was going to be a fag. Not fisted—more of a smack—but still hard enough to knock my bother over and leave a bruise."

"I'm so sorry!" I said, not knowing how else to respond.

"And you want to know what I did? The lame thing I did to help?"

I nodded yes, my hands folded over my heart, feeling the heavy beat of it.

"I quoted John F. Kennedy—"

I think I knew what quote Cody meant, and I whispered, "*If we cannot end now our differences, at least we can make the world safe for diversity.*"

"That's right. And after I said it, my dad was so mad that he hit me, too. Only not quite as hard as he'd hit Carter."

I raised my palms to my mouth in horror. "Cody … Oh, Cody…"

"Willa, my dad says he's going to send Carter to some school, or camp or something, where they will 'straighten him out.' Can you believe that? Come on, *seriously*?" Cody choked out a strangled laugh.

"So, I guess what I'm trying to say is that I really admire you for standing up for the kids who can't stand up for themselves. I *get* that it's a great thing you're doing."

"I—"

Cody held up his hand. "Let me finish, really quick, before this place is crawling with naked girls." Cody smiled as if that wouldn't necessarily be a *bad* thing. "You tell me I dumb it down. Well, you're right. I'm smart, Willa. Super smart. Not as smart as Marley—I don't think there's a single teacher at Triton who's as smart as Marley—but I'm certainly smart enough that I could get into Harvard or Yale if I wanted."

"Then why—"

"You want to know why I don't do well in school? Because I don't *ever* want my dad using me as a comparison to my brother. I don't want Carter to have it any worse than he already does. '*Why can't you be smart like Cody?*' he said, mimicking Mr. Cassidy. '*Why can't you be straight and like girls like your brother Cody?*' So I intentionally don't hand in the work, and I ditch school to go surfing if the waves are up, and yet I still pass with B's."

Cody reached out and took the glasses from my head, gently putting them back on me. He used his finger to press them against the bridge of my nose. And after he did that, he lightly touched the scar above my lip, sending a jolt of electricity through me.

"And the thing with Dakota? Well, you have to admit, Dakota is really hot."

I frowned at Cody. I didn't want to give anything up to Dakota, but some facts are undeniable. Those twins were gorgeous.

"You're right. I'll give you that. Dakota and Dallas are hot." I heard a whistle blow and knew the gym teachers were calling the girls to line up on the field. It was time to go.

Cody got up and reached out to lend me a hand. We both stood on the left side of the benches. "I started going with Dakota not because I liked her that much, but because our parents are friends, and I got the feeling it was expected of me—the way my dad kept inviting her family over and then saying what a good couple we'd make, practically pimping me out. I think by then he had an idea about Carter and he wasn't taking any chances." Cody chopped his fingers through his hair in agitation. "I know we're not a good fit. I *know that*, Willa."

We were almost face-to-face, except that Cody is taller so he had to tip his head down toward me. My body flushed and my stomach churned from his closeness. I knew what Cody was about to do, although I had no idea why he wanted to. My heart and soul screamed yes, but my queasy stomach said … *maybe another time.*

Cody dipped his head down and he closed his eyes, his lips parting and meeting mine. His lips were soft, and they tasted like honey and Burt's Bee's lip balm.

"Mmm …" I moaned, and Cody, mistakenly reading my meaning, pressed his lips harder against mine. "Umm," I groaned, hearing my stomach make some gross churning noises. My throat constricted and I tasted bile, which meant only one thing.

Pushing my hands against Cody's chest, I ran toward the exit doors and over to the trash can, where I leaned over and forcefully vomited inside it. Twice.

"*Wow!* Can't say I saw that one coming," Cody said, hurrying over to me. "Are you okay?" Cody leaned down, concern in his voice, but I quickly waved him away.

"No! I'm fine. *Go!*" I commanded, mortified at the outcome of my first kiss. *And from Cody Cassidy, no less.* I heaved again and let fly another round just as the door opened and the girls' gym class started to file in.

"Cody Cassidy!" Kirby shrieked, carrying a soccer ball tucked under her arm and stopping dead in her tracks forcing the rest of the girls in line to collide into one another. "Lauren! Alexa!" Kirby shouted over the heads of the girls behind her. "Cody's here in the locker room— with Willa!" Kirby transferred her ball to her other arm and peeked over the edge of the trash can. "Ugh, Willa. *Disgusting.* What did you have for lunch? It looks like sushi."

"Bye, Willa. Gotta go!" Cody squeezed out of the door, head down and trying to hide between the girls, just as Coach Patterson caught sight of him. All the girls in line squealed and shrieked in delight over the fact that Cody Cassidy—not just *any* boy, but *the* boy—was in their locker room.

"*Mister* Cassidy!" coach yelled out after him, shaking her head.

Cody stopped running and turned back around. He dropped to one knee to tie his shoe. When he finished, he waved his hat in the air at the coach. Coach waved back and shook her head again. She chuckled, a smile lighting up her masculine face.

Cody Cassidy, the handsome, bright kid with the sweet disposition—the intentional *under*achiever— was a teacher favorite at Triton Middle School. And a darn good kisser.

CHAPTER 15

"At least promise me you'll think about it," Marley said, closing her locker, (a complete disaster for someone usually so detail oriented). Marley and I started walking to our respective homerooms in the next building.

"I'm not going to the dance alone, Marley. That's just lame. Have you not seen the movies? The ones of the dumb girl wearing the pink dress and her black cat-frame glasses, sitting in the metal folding chairs on the side of the gym next to all of the other losers and waiting for a boy to ask her to dance?"

Marley laughed her fairy tinkle laugh.

"Then help me with the sign-in table. Or you can monitor the punch table if you want." Marley waved to some kids passing us in the other direction.

"I am *not* manning the punch table! I can see it now … Dakota spiking the punch and blaming me, or Dakota spilling the entire bowl of punch on my dress, or Dakota—"

"Then ask Robbie to go as your date."

"Uhh … gosh, Marley. I don't know. That's so *Glee*," I said, referring to a TV show that aired from 2009 to 2015 about a group of ambitious misfits who join their high school glee club.

"Good *Glee* or bad *Glee*? Groundbreaking and innovative, or trite and overused?" she asked.

"The second."

So, okay, maybe it was a nice idea, taking Robbie to the dance, but let's be real—it would be nicer for Robbie than it would be for me. Not that I was above Robbie or anything. I'm talking about the mechanics of dancing. The reality of it was there would be little, if any, dancing going on, no matter how easy Kevin McHale—the character who plays Artie in *Glee*—makes it look to rock out to Madonna and "Vogue" while sitting in a wheelchair.

And I know it's never gonna happen, not in a million years—not if I wished on every shooting star in the sky, or blew out a hundred birthday candles, or threw a billion pennies in a fountain, but a part of me wished that Cody would have seen that on the inside I was a pretty decent girl, and maybe have asked me to the dance. Not as his girlfriend, obviously, but as that "buddy" he claims that I am.

Marley and I stood at the doors of our homerooms and said good-bye.

***

"Rob-a-laba!" I greeted Robbie at the lunch tables, super excited to see him and holding a package under my arm. I also said hi to Peter, scarfing down his nachos and nuggets, and thinking I may need to get him a calorie content sheet. Not to be evil, but just so he could make good conscious decisions regarding the food choices offered in the school cafeteria.

Robbie twitched and jerked in his wheelchair, happy to see me. "Will ... aahh ... laa .. baa," he stammered, not getting that it didn't work with my name. He would have needed to go with Willa-*waba*, maybe.

"Whaa … daat?" He pointed to the package under my arm. When I say he "pointed" I actually mean he "gestured," and it was with his shoulder more than anything.

I held out the package. "This, my friend, is your ticket to fame. You can thank me later. And just remember when you've got your own Vegas stand-up act at Circus Circus or MGM or whatever hotels are still around—I want my cut." I held it out to him. "Go ahead. Open it." I placed the brown paper wrapped package on his tray top and stood back.

"Willa, that's just plain mean." Cody had come over from the beautiful side of the lunch pond to wallow in the marsh with us ugly ducklings and he stood there frowning at me.

Robbie didn't seem to mind. He smiled a crooked smile, happy as could be that I'd given him a present that he couldn't possibly open.

"My presentation is meant to be symbolic," I explained, not letting Cody dampen my excitement.

"Here, dude. Let me help you," Cody reached out to tear the paper from the package.

And since all kids are suckers for what's inside wrapped gifts, kids began to come over from their lunch tables to investigate. Within minutes, we had a big crowd, including Marley, who came over with all *The Armada* kids.

Cody finished tearing off all the paper, and we all stood staring at a box that looked like it contained a computer keyboard. "U-Talk," Cody read from the box. "Voice synthesizer and communication device."

"Ohh, Spider-girl," Marley softly said, tears filling her eyes.

"What is it?" Kirby asked, leaning forward to look closer at the picture printed on the box.

Seeing Marley tear up made my eyes water, and I croaked out, "It's Robbie's voice. Now everyone will be able to understand him and get to hear his great jokes."

It may have been that the wind suddenly kicked up, spreading the dust and the dirt, but I could swear that Cody's eyes sparkled just a bit. He cleared his throat before speaking. "Let's get this puppy fired up!"

It took a little time trying to figure out how it all worked: the joystick, the screen, and the tiny speaker, with Cody following the directions that seemed to be printed in every language but English. Eventually he got it all put together and he patiently explained to Robbie how it worked.

"That's just the basic settings." Cody arranged the components onto the front of his tray. "You'll have to spend some time customizing the program. I think you even have choices on what accent you'd like. If it were me, I'd pick the one with the guy that sounds British. *Bond. James Bond*," he mimicked, "*and I'll have mine shaken, not stirred.*" Cody smiled wide. "So what do you think, buddy? Think you can handle it?"

We all moved closer to Robbie, waiting for his first (synthesized) words.

Robbie used his better hand and did as Cody instructed. "**I-think-so**," Robbie said, the words coming out clearly, loud and strong, although somewhat mechanical and sounding a lot like Stephen Hawking.

"Cody says you have some really funny jokes,

Robbie." Brylee said. "Can you tell us one?"

"Yeah, Robbie, tell us a joke," Dylan said.

The air suddenly froze and all the birds flew away as Dakota made her way over to the group. Not that anyone noticed the change in the atmosphere or the sudden migration of the birds, besides me. Everyone was still staring at Robbie.

Robbie used the joystick to spell out the words, and his new voice boomed, **"How-do-you-make-seven-an-even-number?"** His leg suddenly jerked in a spasm, but no one seemed to mind.

"I don't know. How?" Brylee asked. Dakota rolled her eyes and Dallas copied her. Robbie was too busy with the joystick to notice.

"Take-the-S-out," Robbie said after a moment, a huge smile on his face that warmed my heart and made me tear up again.

Jax howled with laughter. "Take the S out! *You take the S out!* The guy is killing me." He nudged Brylee with his elbow.

"*Seriously?* Oh, please," Dakota sneered, looking at all our faces before turning to Jax. "And what have you been smoking, Jax? That joke is so, like, second grade."

Robbie's hand was furiously working the joystick. **"Then-here's-one-for-you-Dakota,"** he said, his body lurching to the left before coming back to center. Dakota took a step back. **"What-do-Tupperware-and-a-walrus-have-in-common?"**

Dakota shook her head, indicating she hadn't a clue.

"Give-up?" Everyone waited for the punch line while Robbie constructed the answer. Soon enough, the Stephen Hawking voice said, **"They-both-like-a-ti ..."**

"And I think that's quite enough for now," Marley said as she started to wheel Robbie away from the crowd, against the wishes of most of the boys who wanted to hear how the joke ended, figuring it had to be naughty.

"That's disgusting," Dakota said, scrunching her face in a way that was less than flattering. Ten to one, she hadn't a clue what the punch line was anyway. She turned to me. "How'd you get the money to pay for that, Willa? What, did you have to sell your body to science or something? Donate your *brain*? Aren't those voice things, like, a thousand dollars?"

The U-Talk cost much more than that, but it was worth every penny to help give Robbie a voice.

"Yeah, Willa," Cody said. "Where'd you get the money? Did your parents give it to you?"

Yeah, right.

"I sold my eraser collection," I said quietly, hoping that no one could hear the answer but Cody.

No good. The fruit bat heard me, and she shrieked, "You sold your *eraser* collection? Hear that, everyone? Willa has an ERASER collection!"

Not anymore.

Petra agreed to buy my eraser collection to add to hers. Seems like I had some really valuable ones that she couldn't get her hands on. Probably because they were produced from some sort of toxic materials now outlawed in every major country, but making them super rare because of it.

"Yeah, Dakota!" I snarked back at her. "So I had an eraser collection that I sold to buy Robbie a voice synthesizer. So what? Sue me for trying to do something nice for someone!"

Cody was staring at me with an expression of … I don't know, but it was something good. Admiration, maybe. Pride?

"*Ohhh* … Miss Goody-Two-Shoes," Dakota sing-songed.

"Shut up, Dakota! Just shut up for once in your life!" Cody whirled towards her. "I'm sick of you. We're all sick of you acting like you're so much better than everyone else. Quit being so mean all the time. It isn't attractive. In fact, it makes you ugly."

Dakota struggled to open her purse and find her compact, opening it to check to see if what Cody said was true and she had suddenly become … *gasp!* … ugly.

"I meant it figuratively, you dummy," Cody said, shaking his head as if he couldn't believe he'd ever gone out with her. (That's pure conjecture on my part.) "I'm so over you."

Dakota, shocked at Cody's words, started to sputter a rebuttal, but instead, she choked on her gum. Dallas pounded her sister on the back until Dakota managed to swallow it down.

The bell rang and everyone started gathering their backpacks and their books, except for Cody, who never seemed to carry any as part of his rebel-with-a-cause routine.

All *The Armada* kids came over to give me kudos and some of the cool kids too: Brylee, Keiran, and Hallie. Jax looked as if he was going to come over, but then the wind picked up and blew a plastic baggie into the air and he ran off to chase after it.

Armada Audrey touched me on the arm. "Marley told us your suggestion, Willa, and we think it's a great idea; Robbie's own joke column in the paper. *Wise Cracks*, wasn't that the name you suggested for it?" Audrey hugged her books to her chest. "It's a fabulous idea, Willa. Absolutely stellar. I'm sure the paper will be better than ever. Thank you." She smiled at me while the other kids, Omar, Amir, and Rebekka nodded in agreement and offered up their thanks as well. They said *adios*, (that's good-bye in Spanish, although they said it in English) moving past me to head in the direction of the science building.

And speaking of thanks … There was someone that really deserved mine.

CHAPTER 16

Cody was halfway to the gym as I rushed out after him.

"Cody, wait!" I yelled, my backpack an anchor slowing me down, or proving that I'm just super unfit, and I need to put more of an effort into running and exercise.

Cody stopped, waiting for me to catch up. When I finally did, my hair had come loose from its ponytail, and I was out of breath and sweating like a banshee.

"How's P.E. going for you, Chicago?" Cody chuckled. "About the same as math?" I didn't mind the sarcasm half as much as I minded him calling me Chicago. I wanted Cody to see me as me. Willa Shisbey, the girl he kissed in the locker room before she hurled her lunch.

I dropped my backpack on the ground and then leaned over to put my hands on my knees, trying to catch my breath. "Thanks to you ... *gasp, gasp, gasp* ... I'm doing much better in math ... *huff, huff, huff* ... I just may eek out a B on my report card ... *pant, pant, pant* ... unlike you."

When I was finally able to breathe without feeling like I needed a respirator, I stood upright.

Cody dimpled. "Me? Naw. Just watch. I'll end up with a B. I'll do some extra credit work, and I'll ace the finals. If that doesn't work, I'll bring Mrs. Deejet some flowers and maybe write her a sappy poem about what a great teacher she is and how because of her I have a newfound passion for math. Don't worry about me. I'll pass that class with a decent grade."

But I did worry about Cody. I worried about him constantly. I worried not only about his grades, but also about how his father treated him (now that he'd shared that his dad had a bad temper). I worried if Cody was sleeping well, or taking his vitamins. I worried if there was too much mercury in the fish he was eating, or if he was wearing his sweater when it was cold out. I worried that Cody might have cavities just starting to form (daughter of a dentist thing), and that someday he might develop male pattern baldness (but I'd love him anyway—bald or not). But most of all, I worried that now that Cody had helped me understand math, and that he'd done such a great job helping people to accept Robbie ... that he would no longer want to be my friend.

Cody stood patiently, waiting for me to speak. We were both going to be late for class, but who cared?

"I wanted to thank you, Cody, for helping me. Without you, I never could have done it."

"I don't know about that." Cody pulled up the hood of his sweatshirt so that it covered his hair. "I'm pretty sure you can do whatever you set your mind to, there, *Spider-girl*. Isn't that what Marley called you?" Cody studied me for a moment. "It fits. The ability to cling tenaciously to most surfaces ... A subconscious precognitive sense of danger—"

"Stop when you get to sticking people to my back, and the ability to crawl on walls and ceilings. Because if you want to know the truth, I have a freakish fear of spiders, and it's all I can do to take

Marley's comparison as a compliment." Cody laughed and dug his hands into his pockets. "Seriously, though, Cody, without you, and your power—"

"Oh, yeah, *right*." He cut me off. "My power of *popularity*," he said sarcastically. "That ranks right up there with superhuman strength and stellar reflexes. I'm a regular superhero." And the way that Cody said it, almost smirking, it seemed as if he were condemning himself.

"But you helped," I pointed out.

"Naw. It was you, Willa. All you." The tardy bell rang, and we continued to stand there. "You think I would have thought of helping Robbie if it weren't for you? I probably wouldn't have given him a second thought. Not that I'd be mean or anything. But I would have seen him sitting there and thought to myself, tough break. Or worse, I probably would have thought *better him than me*. How sick is that? I'd have looked at him and been thankful it wasn't me trapped in that chair."

Cody pulled his hands out of his pockets and pushed back the hood of his sweatshirt, chopping his fingers through his hair. He turned and looked off towards the bleachers. "Would I have stood up for him like you did? Sold my eraser collection to buy him a voice? No. I would have done exactly what I've done to stand up to people about my brother being gay. I would have done *nothing*." Cody turned and began to walk away.

"Cody, wait!" I caught up to him and reached out my hand to touch his arm. "Why did you kiss me? I'm not pretty. I'm not popular. Then why? I need to know why you kissed me." And I did need to know. Because as much as I'd replayed it over in my mind 132 times, I still didn't know why Cody kissed me.

Cody sighed ... a sigh much too deep for an eighth grader who has it all.

"I like you, Willa," he said.

I filled in the blank, ... *as a friend.*

"You're a good person." ...

You're ugly, I translated.

"You're funny and you're kind." ...

A total loser and not my type.

"But I don't want to be those things," I rushed out. "I want to be cool and popular, like you are."

Hearing how lame it sounded, I backtracked. "I mean … yes, I want to be good and kind—and funny has its moments …" I trailed off.

"*Really*, Willa? You think being popular should be your highest aspiration? Think about it. What will people remember Dakota for after we graduate?"

"For being gorgeous?"

"Exactly," Cody said, the words stinging. "And what will they say when she arrives at some school reunion twenty years from now and she's no longer gorgeous? 'There's Dakota Duncan, the girl who used to be pretty.' But if *you* went to that reunion, what would those very same people say about you?"

I kicked at a piece of dried gum embedded into the blacktop, my eyes down. "I don't know. 'There's that nerdy girl with the weird memory problem?'"

"No, Willa. That's not what they'd say. After today, what they would say is 'There's Wilhelmina Shisbey, that nice girl from Chicago who made a difference in someone's life.' Popularity is *nothing*, Willa. At least not in the grand scheme of things. It's temporary—just ask any president that gets a 24-percent approval rating after only a couple years in office," he said as an afterthought. "But let me name you just a few people in history who were known for kindness and see if their names don't ring a bell. Mother Theresa, Gandhi, The Dalai Lama, even J.C. himself. *Those* are the people we remember, not the Dakota and Dallas Duncans of the world."

Sure. Cody was right. But still… Yes, I know, it's good to be kind, and that supposedly beauty comes from within—although Diane says that's ridiculous, no woman is naturally pretty, and that beauty doesn't come from within, beauty actually comes from the makeup counter at Nordstrom.

I glanced down at my watch and knew I was going to be in big trouble. I don't know about Cody, but I was going to have to play the "I got my period" card.

"I understand what you're telling me, Cody, but what about the saying 'Nice guys finish last'?"

Cody leaned toward me and he whispered in my ear, his breath warm and sweet. *"Sometimes it's all just a matter of who's waiting for you at the end of the race."*

CHAPTER 17

Don't believe the fairy tales and the happily ever afters. In real life, the cute boy doesn't ditch the cute girl for the orphan born with the messed up face and the knack for remembering dates.

It was a long shot, I know, but part of me thought that there was some message in Cody's "end of the race" teaser. I must have misread him, because the next day Cody acted the same as ever. And not only that, but I sorta thought that after I'd done such a nice thing for Robbie that I'd get to school and there would be some recognition for my generosity.

I'm not saying I expected a parade in my honor or anything. Not that it wouldn't have been super cool—a float with a huge likeness of me made out of flower petals and seeds like in the Rose Parade, and maybe some confetti and streamers raining down as I passed by, and the school band playing "For She's a Jolly Good Fellow" or maybe the USC fight song, "Fight On."

Or, if not a parade, then at least an acknowledgment, some shout out in the principal's announcements during homeroom, or maybe a bouquet of congratulations balloons sent by a singing telegram during science or math class.

But there was nothing. No "Vote Willa for Dance Diva" (some lame thing they have for the dance) pasted on my locker. No one slipping invitations to their slumber parties in my hand as they passed me in the hallway, or a suggestion I sit at the cool kid table at lunch. Nothing.

Okay, so maybe "nothing" is being a bit unappreciative. I did get a nice hug from Marley, and a wonderful letter from Robbie's parents thanking me and inviting me over for dinner some Friday night for Sabbath. (Which, FYI, is not the name of an actual dish, but rather the Jewish religious ritual of serving the specially prepared meal.)

But that's the thing about life. You do the right thing just because it's the right thing to do. Because, if you think about it, except for an action doll made in their likeness, (and maybe tons of money if they get a piece of all that merchandising dough) what does a superhero really get but a handshake and a "thanks" by the mayor—and maybe the key to the city?

***

"What's the word, nerd? Are we going to do this, or what?" Olivia came into my room bearing an arsenal of beauty products for the second phase of what she called the "Turn Willa Into a Girl" project, in preparation of tonight's dance. The first phase started off rocky, (as in, it took two long hours to find the perfect dress in Olivia's closet), and there was a chance this part might take just as long. No wonder I don't go to dances. Who has the extra four hours it takes to get ready for one?

We must have gone through half a dozen dresses in Olivia's closet before finding the perfect one. Here are some of the misses: The Posh V-Back—a slinky red dress with a plunging back that almost exposed the crack in my rear end, (and would have if I hadn't been wearing my Saturday panties on a Friday.) Then there was The Plunging V-Neckline—a slinky dress in shocking pink with ... are you ready? ... a plunging V-neckline! That sucker plunged right past my bellybutton and into Saturday. There was also The Cross-Back Skater Dress, an electric-blue dress with a dozen straps crisscrossing the back of it and the likes not seen in public since the last Winter Olympics. We finally found a hit with a modest seashell-pink sleeveless dress with a sequined bodice and flared skirt that Olivia says is Blaine's, that she left behind the week before. We paired the dress with Darling Floral D'Orsay Flats, and they *were*, indeed, darling!

"Explain to me again why you're going to be a chaperone. Isn't that sort of like the fox watching the hen house?" I said to Olivia as she used a hair claw to get my hair out of the way so she could play Picasso. She told me to close my eyes, and she slathered on something she said was an eye shadow *base* (not to be confused with the eye shadow itself that to me looked exactly like the base).

"I already told you. The cheerleaders are doing it as a sort of public service." She stroked on my eyelids some sort of liquid eyeliner before changing her mind and taking it off with a Q-tip.

I kept my eyes closed as instructed but kept talking. "Public service, you say? Hmm. What you mean to say is you all couldn't quite stomach the thought of serving the homeless, so you thought you'd man the punch table at the middle school dance instead."

"Exactly." Olivia swept some blush on my cheeks with a huge brush that looked like it needed a dustpan to go with it. "*Good ...*" Olivia said more to herself than to me. "Oh yeah, this is good." She brushed some more before moving on to the mascara. "Remember, no glasses. No matter what. No glasses. No matter if you're stumbling around like a blind man in a snowstorm, just keep those stupid things off."

"But what if I need to see?"

"Quit exaggerating, Harry Potter. You can see fine. You just won't be able to *read* anything. I'll loan you my cute clutch purse so that you'll have them in case of emergency." Olivia finished with the eyes and then went for the lips, applying Baby Lips Electro lip balm in Strike a Rose and then finishing it with a clear gloss. When she was finished, she took two steps back and held her thumb up eyeing her creation. (And probably having no clue that an artist does that to compare proportions.) "Now for the hair," she said.

Twenty minutes later, painted, sprayed, and lacquered within an inch of my life, Olivia squealed, "*Omigod!* I am such a genius! A total miracle worker. Just look at you! You look amazing!" Olivia jumped up and down, clapping her hands. "Just wait until Cody sees you. That little so-in-so Dakota Duncan doesn't have a chance." Olivia's eyes dropped to my chest. "Well, except for that." She pointed. "You sure you don't want to stuff your bra? I have some silicone things you put inside to give you lift. They work really well."

"Thanks, but no. I think you actually need something to lift. Besides," I said, "I think that's false advertising and there are laws against it. Bait and switch, maybe." I slowly walked over to the mirrored wardrobe doors, and I stared. And I stared some more, as my eyes began to tear.

"Don't you cry! Willa, don't you dare cry, I didn't use waterproof mascara." Olivia came over to stand next to me. "You look great, kid," she said, putting her arm around my shoulder and hugging me to her side.

And I did look great. Pretty, even. Olivia had used cover-up to hide the scar above my lip, and the blush sculpted my cheeks, making my face less round. The eye makeup was just enough (despite feeling as if I had on a ton) and emphasized the shape of my eyes, although they were still brown, and not blue, like I'd prefer. The pink lipstick glistened, and the lip-liner had given me pouty lips I didn't know I owned. My straight brown hair had been gently teased at the back to add some height, and Olivia had used a wide-barrel curling iron to give my hair some "movement," whatever that is, parting it on the side and securing it with a glittery pink headband.

I stood there mute. Shocked into silence at the transformation. This wasn't me. It would never be me. It felt strange and alien, both exhilarating and scary at the same time. It wasn't me at all. But I'd have three hours. Three hours to pretend to be something I wasn't, before turning back into the pumpkin, or the mouse, or the scullery maid.

"Come on, girl," Olivia encouraged. "Let's show those yahoos what Chicago is made of."

***

"Willa!" Marley exclaimed as I "swam" my way over to her. The dance theme was "Under the Sea," and we were supposed to be underwater, with the school gym transformed into a Technicolor version of the ocean floor. "You look amazing! Just wait until Cody sees you. He won't be able to keep his eyes off you. I know I sure can't." Marley leaned toward me and gave me a great big hug. An eighth grader, some tall guy that I didn't know, gave us a "look," but one that said a chick-chick hug wasn't something he was necessarily against. He gave us a wink and passed by us to go inside.

In true Triton sprit, Marley was dressed sort of mermaid-ish—and not for the first time since I've known her. She wore a pink, green, and purple iridescent scarf dress, and orange flats, although they did have a green seashell glued to the top, so they kinda matched. She'd given up the pigtails for French braids, and they were secured by rubber bands that had tiny glittery starfish on them.

"Come on!" Marley pulled me by the hand and took me inside, where tons of kids had already assembled, all waiting for the music to start. "Robbie's waiting for you."

Robbie wasn't my date, though. I didn't have a date for the dance. Instead I was going *stag*. (As an adverb it means "without a partner at a social gathering.") Robbie was actually going to be both the MC and the DJ for the dance, and I was his assistant. This worked out well for both of us, since I don't dance. If you saw the size of my feet in relationship to my height, you'd know why. My dad says someday the ratio will work itself out and he'll teach me to fox trot. As if!

I butterfly-stroked my way through hanging streamers and giant squid and over to where Robbie had his table set up. "Rob-O!" I leaned in to give him a quick hug and breaking rule number two of the dance; no full-body contact. Not that I had full-body contact with Robbie, it was more shoulder contact than anything else, but the teachers were constantly on vigil for anything that remotely could be construed as boy/girl touching. And rule number one of the dance? No twerking. There will be no thrusting of hips.

"**Will-O!**" Robbie shouted back in a new voice I hadn't yet heard him use. It was a bit surprising, as it was decidedly black. Not that there's anything wrong with that. Just sayin'.

"Lil G?" I asked, and thinking U-Talk must have expanded voice options.

"**JAZZY-J**," Robbie said.

"Oh, sure. Yes, definitely." I nodded. "You look nice, Robbie." And he did. He was wearing black pants and one of those T-shirts that have a tuxedo printed on them. For once, he wasn't wearing the orange beanie, and in a way, it seemed as though he was missing something to complete his outfit.

Robbie eyed my outfit. His mouth hung open a bit and a thin line of drool dribbled from his lips. It might have been because of how nice I looked. Then again, maybe not. "May I?" I asked him, before dabbing the corner of his mouth and then pushing the napkin inside his cup holder.

"You look beautiful, Willa," Robbie said, and coming from JAZZY-J, it made me blush, because, come on, just how many times is JAZZY-J going to tell a thirteen-year-old from Triton Middle School that she's beautiful? How about … *never*!

I started arranging the CDs in the order of Robbie's printed playlist (which meant that I just shuffled them around because I couldn't see a thing without my glasses) and made sure that all the speakers were plugged in and ready to roll.

"It's all smoke and mirrors," I explained. "This isn't me. In fact, if it gets too hot in here, my entire face is going to melt into one giant puddle. I'll just be a headless body in a pink dress. Besides, you're just saying that because you're my friend, and you owe me, like, your entire life," I joked.

"I don't think that's it. Why don't we ask *him*?" Robbie jerked his shoulder forward.

I glanced across the folding table and came face-to-face with Cody. My stomach lurched.

"Wow! Willa?" The way he said it made it sound like a question.

"Yeah. It's me. I'd offer you my driver's license

as proof, but I don't have it on me." I pointed to the other side of the gym. "My sister's over there somewhere. She can vouch for me. This is all her doing. Some sort of science experiment on how much makeup one girl can wear before her face drops off from the sheer weight of it."

I was yammering, I know, but Cody was looking at me with, I don't know, amazement, maybe, or something like *yowzer!* And the thought of that somehow suddenly made me feel depressed. *Lipstick on a pig,* I remember Diane repeating on September 9, 2008, during the presidential campaign. For all of Olivia's hard work, it was still just lipstick on a pig.

"*Mister Cassidy!*" Ms. Merchant, the assistant principal, bustled over to us. "How many times do I need to remind you that hats are not allowed on campus?"

"But it's after hours, Ms. M," Cody complained, handing the black fedora with the gray band over to her. The hat was a perfect complement to Cody's outfit of black corduroy pants and a navy blue and gray button-down short-sleeved shirt.

Ms. Merchant took the hat and placed in on top of one of the tall speakers behind the table where Robbie had his equipment set up. "I don't want you setting a precedent," she continued. "If I let one student break the rules, the next thing you know, someone else will break the rules. And so it goes."

"Resulting in total anarchy," I whispered. "Today a fedora, tomorrow a top hat. Just where will it all end?"

"Excuse me, Wilhelmina?" she quipped.

"I said, jeez, look at the time." I pretended to glance at the watch that I wasn't wearing. "Robbie, pump up the jams!"

And like a good friend, Robbie did. Just about blowing the skirt right off of Ms. Merchant. She covered her ears with her hands and hurried off to untangle a couple of kids slow dancing to techno rock.

Just then, the two eels, Dakota and Dallas, the minions of the sea witch, slithered toward us, their strapless sequined tops shiny in the light.

And before I proceed, may I just take a moment to ask what brain-dead moron wears an elasticized strapless dress to a dance? This is a dance! Where, you know, you're actually supposed to *dance*? As in, jump up and down? Maybe shimmy, or bend down, even? I had half a mind to reach across and just yank that sucker down, just to prove my point.

"Willa?" Dakota and Dallas gasped at the same time.

Oh, come on! *Seriously?* Somebody hand me a piece of paper and a black marker so I can make a sign that says *Yes, I am Willa Shisbey. I will self-destruct in three hours.*

Dakota was the first to recover. "Well, that just proves why they use ugly people on all those makeover shows. Because the end result is so dramatic," she finished, just as Olivia made her way over to me from the punch table to stand by my side.

"Why, you little—"

"WELCOME, TRITON!" JAZZY-J boomed, drowning out Olivia's words. I held fast to the back of Olivia's shirt to keep her from ripping Dakota's nicely styled blonde hair off her head. **"Let's get this party started!"** Robbie yelled. Everyone cheered and began to dance, except for our little group and *The Armada* kids, who were also the organizers of the event and far too busy to enjoy themselves.

"You!" Olivia said, pointing to Dakota, "need to get out of my face. Why don't you go get yourself some punch? Your face is all dry-looking. Dehydrated, even." Olivia squinted her eyes at Dakota as if she were assessing her lack of proper pH balance. Then she turned to Cody. "And *you*— surfer boy—you need to ask my sister to dance."

"But … I …" I stammered. "I can't. I mean …" I turned toward Cody, who was holding his hand out to me. "Who … who will help Robbie?"

"I will," Olivia said. She glanced at the small spot of drool on his chin. "I said, I got it!" And to prove it, Olivia reached inside the cup holder and wiped Robbie's chin. She didn't ask his permission, but the way Robbie blushed and smiled at Olivia, I don't think he minded. "It's you and me kid," she said to him, giving him a fist bump. "You're gonna have to cut my sister loose. Looks like I'm your sidekick for the night."

Olivia dismissed us saying there was something important she needed to tell Blaine, manning the punch table on the other side of the gym. Olivia pulled out her phone and texted Blaine, who must have gotten the message because she waved from across the room.

Cody pulled me to the dance floor. "What about Dakota?" I said.

"What about her?"

We both turned toward the punch table just in time to see Blaine hand Dakota a full glass of punch. Suddenly, Sienna, the other cheerleader, bumped into Blaine, forcing Blaine forward, the entire cup of red fruit punch splattering down the front of Dakota's yellow dress. Even from across the room we heard the shrieking. Dallas tried to help, but instead of dabbing, she wiped. She wiped so hard it pulled the front of Dakota's dress down to her waist, revealing a cherry-patterned bra that looked to be stuffed with those silicone cutlets Olivia wanted me to try. All the kids around her began to laugh and point, and Dakota started to cry, and in a way, I felt sorry for her.

"What goes around comes around," Cody said sagely, while he stood waiting for the right break in the music to start dancing.

"Yo! Listen up everybody," Rob-J announced. **"It's time to announce the winner of tonight's Dance Diva award. As a reminder, the contestants must be present to win. Let's bring up one of Huntington Harbor's favorite cheerleaders, Blaine Banks, to announce the winner."**

Blaine bounced over to where Robbie and Olivia stood. Olivia quickly whispered something into her ear and Blaine nodded. "Hi, y'all," Blaine said, acknowledging the applause. "The Dance Diva award is for the young lady who most exemplifies the spirit of Triton Middle School. It can be in dress, in personality, or in deed." Blaine accepted the envelope from Ms. Merchant. "And the winner is …" Robbie played a synthesized version of a drum roll. Blaine's eyes scanned the crowd. "She's not here," she said to Ms. Merchant. Ms. Merchant must have instructed her to go to the second name. Blaine nodded, her eyes searching the crowd again. "Uh, I think she left with her sister."

A murmur started in the crowd, everyone knowing that it had to be both Dakota and Dallas who won first and second place. I cut my eyes toward Cody and he shrugged. People turned to stare at Brylee, who was the next most popular girl in school. Brylee blushed and hesitantly started walking toward the table.

Blaine stole a quick glance at Olivia before saying, "And the winner of tonight's Dance Diva award goes to ... *Wilhelmina Shisbey!* Congratulations, Willa!" And with that, Blaine tore up the paper into little bits, throwing them into the air like confetti.

I stood glued to my spot while around me the kids cheered and applauded, Marley coming at me in full skip. "I knew you would win, Willa! I just knew it! I voted for you. And all *The Armada* kids, too. And, of course, Robbie did," she prattled on, giving me a tight hug.

"I voted for you, Willa," Cody said, "and I'm pretty sure Jax and Dylan did, too."

And still I stood, stunned. I didn't believe it. Not for a minute. I saw the look Olivia gave Blaine. There was no way I could have won unless they cheated. No way.

Cody took my hand in his and started heading toward the DJ table. "Come on, Willa. I think they're waiting to give you a crown. I think it came from Burger King, but hey, it's still a crown."

This was the fairy tale ending. But it didn't feel right. Cody, who was only interested in me now because I was suddenly pretty-ish. And winning Dance Diva because my sister cheated for me.

Like a girl in a trance, I let Blaine put the crown on my head, and I smiled a fake smile at the crowd and waved pitifully. I even let Cody pull me onto the dance floor, where he put his hands on my waist, instructing me to put my hands on his shoulders. "I can't dance, Cody. I don't know how," I said, my voice not sounding like mine. Or if it did, sounding as if I were about to cry.

"That's okay. I do. It's like surfing. It's all about the balance." Cody's face went serious, and his eyes grew dark. "Can I tell you something without you getting mad at me?" His hands tightened on my waist and he swayed gently from side to side.

"Sure."

"I like you better the other way."

"What way?"

"The natural way. The Willa way, where your personality shines through. Without all that fake makeup and that gooey lip gloss. Guys hate that stuff. And did you get contacts? Where are your glasses?"

It was as if I had been stuck at the bottom of the ocean, held by some sort of anchor of self-doubt and unworthiness. But then I broke free, and I swam to the top, reaching the surface of the water.

Cody did like me for me! He liked the nerdy girl with the oversized glasses same as her dad's. The kid with the super memory and the fondness for sweetened breakfast cereals. The girl who was nice and kind (Cody's words), who did a good deed, and was voted Dance Diva because of it. *Maybe.*

But more importantly, Cody made me realize that I didn't need a boy to like me in order to feel better about myself. Gosh, I'd take one best friend like Marley over a hundred Codys. A true friend, someone who corrected me when I needed it, and loved me unconditionally. A friend who taught me that we're not born to fit in, we're born to stand *out*.

I leaned forward and I kissed Cody on the cheek. "Thank you, Cody. Thank you so much!" I dropped my hands from him and rushed across the dance floor and over to my sister, who stood next to Robbie tapping her feet in time to the music.

"I need to talk to you!" I grabbed Olivia's arm and pulled her to the side. "Did you cheat for me?" I demanded, although there wasn't much oomph to it. After all, if Olivia cheated, it was because she loves me.

"Of course not!" she denied.

"Swear?"

"Define cheating."

"I knew it! I knew I couldn't have won unless you cheated for me."

"It's not what you think, Willa."

"Then explain it to me, Olivia."

"It's like this …" Olivia pushed her hair behind her ear. "Obviously, that no-good twit of a sister to Denver was the winner. But I swear, Willa, I didn't know it when I had Blaine dump punch all over her.

I also didn't know Dallas won second-place and that she'd leave with Dakota. If that were us, I'd have stayed."

"You don't say."

Olivia ignored my sarcasm. "It was a tie between you and Brylee. Really. A total tie. But when Blaine and Sienna were tabulating the votes, there was one ballot that had *both* of your names, and they were both sort of erased, but it seemed to them that your name was the bolder one, the one that may have been their real choice for Dance Diva. So they went with their gut. They went with the girl who deserved to win. And that's you, Willa. You deserved it. It took you most of your miserable little life to build up that eraser collection and you sold it to buy a voice synthesizer for a kid you barely know."

And the way that Olivia said it, about me and my miserable little life, with tears in her eyes and her voice breaking, I knew it was the sincerest form of flattery. Because, after all, this is *Olivia* we're talking about.

"Come on! Look at what you've accomplished." Olivia pointed to Robbie, cutting and bobbing in time to the music while around him all the kids in school danced and had a good time.

Cody arrived just then and he put his arm around my waist. My stomach did a flip-flop. I might not need a boy to validate my worth, but seriously, this was *Cody Cassidy*, the first boy I ever kissed. There wasn't a person at Triton, staff included, immune to his charm.

"Look at him, Willa," Olivia said, pointing to Robbie, who now sported black sunglasses someone had put on him. "He's totally cool."

Cody spied his hat still sitting on top of the speaker. He jogged over to get it and then beckoned me over to join him. Taking my hand, we walked over to Robbie, totally stylin' in his dark sunglasses and nodding in time to the music. Letting go of my hand, Cody took his black fedora and ceremoniously placed the hat on top of Robbie's head.

"There you go, dude. Now you're lookin' sharp." Cody glanced my way and gave me a wink.

"*Oh, Cody*," I said, wanting to thank him, but not finding the words.

Cody shrugged, his lips tugging into that smile that made my legs turn to cooked linguini.

Robbie used his joystick. **"Thank you,"** his synthesizer said for him. Robbie gave us a modified thumbs-up, a wide grin on his face. He dropped his hand and wrote some more. **"Now I'm cool!"** his JAZZY-J voice said.

"Hey, no worries." Cody returned the thumbs up.

Cody and I stepped away from the table to give Robbie space to do his thing. We stood against the wall and watched him. Not the kid with a disability. But Robbie Wise—the new cool kid at Triton, the rebel in the hat, wearing the biggest smile you've ever seen, using his joystick and announcing the next song.

"I hope Ms. Merchant doesn't make him ditch the hat. He looks great in it," Cody remarked.

And I suddenly recalled June 28, 2009—a Sunday—the warm sun streaming through the kitchen window as I sat eating a bowl of Lucky Charms and reading *Calvin and Hobbes* in the funnies section of the morning paper.

"I know, right? Because, *'what fun is it being cool—if you can't wear a sombrero?'*"

A favor — pretty please...

Do you enjoy reading and writing as much as I do? Would you like to see your words in print for all the world to see? Then here's your chance. All you have to do is write and post a quick REVIEW of Confessions of a Nerdy Girl: *NERDY EVER AFTER* to Amazon, Goodreads, or the retail source of this book.

Whether short and sweet — or long and lyrical, I'd love to hear your thoughts!

Thanks so much,

XOXOXO

Linda

SAMPLE CHAPTERS:

Confessions of a Nerdy Girl: TOP SECRET

Diary #1

March 1, 7:09 P.M.

~~Dear Diary,~~

Ugh! That looks even dumber on paper than it sounds out loud.

~~Dear Journal,~~
Nope.
~~Dear Ledger,~~ Definitely not. Too CPA-ish.

Notebook? Chronicle? Log? (Log? That's ripe. What is this—Star Trek?)

Who would ever think it's this hard to begin a

diary? The chances of this thing working out are pretty slim if I can't get past the first two words. And even if I figure out what to name you — you are a "you" right? Isn't that why I'm supposed to start off with a greeting ... Dear so and so, because you're like some imaginary or invisible friend? Then what? I pour out all the details of my crappy life so I can get even more depressed when I see it all in black and white? As if living through it in real time isn't bad enough?

Maybe I'm looking at this the wrong way. Maybe having a diary is supposed to be more like I'm talking to myself, a way for my conscious to communicate with my subconscious or something. If that's the case, then I guess I should start off with the words, "Dear Me."

Oh my GOSH! I am sooo overthinking this! But then I'm clinically OCD, so I overthink everything. Who CARES what I start with? It's a diary for Pete's sake, not a Master's thesis. This book even has a corny pastel cover that says WARNING! DO NOT READ! PRIVATE PROPERTY! (which of course just begs it be read by any Tom, Dick or Harry, or in my case, my sister Olivia.) It even comes with the prerequisite lock and key, which is a total joke because it's so flimsy any five-year-old with a paperclip could pick it.

My dad (he's actually my adoptive dad, but he's real to me) gave me this diary because he says he's noticed a change in me, and not for the better I'm guessing, and he thought that if I got my feelings out on paper maybe I'd get a better sense of "perspective." See things in a "different light."

He's right about the change. There'd be a change in you too if your dad came home one day and told you to start packing your stuff because the family was moving to Huntington Beach, California, in two months.

Now, I know what you're thinking: California! The beach! Whoo hoo! Sunshine. Surfing. Bikinis. Tanned legs and blond highlights in your hair. Cute boys on skateboards, or surfboards, or boogie boards. But as they say at the Italian restaurant around the corner of my house when you ask for cheddar cheese to put on your spaghetti—fuggedaboutit.

First off, I hate the sun and it's fair to say the feeling is mutual. Ten minutes in the sun and my paper-white skin gets lobster red, until eventually it peels off in gross tissue-sized layers leaving behind, wanna guess? More white skin.

Second, I have astigmatism, so I wear thick glasses and can't see worth a darn without them, and I know for a fact the Pacific Ocean has sharks. I also know it has dolphins, but without my glasses (and maybe even with them) I'd be hard-pressed to tell the difference. A fin is a fin is a fin, especially when the saltwater is burning the crapola out of your half-blind retinas.

Third, I try NOT to go around half-naked in public because of all the hair on my arms and legs. It's black and long, and against my white skin ... Well, I'm sure you get the unattractive picture. Diane—my adoptive mom (who will never be real to me) won't let me shave my legs until next year.

She says she didn't let Olivia, her gorgeous but insanely evil daughter, shave until she was in middle school, so I can't either. I argued that in Olivia's case it didn't matter because Olivia has blond hair on her head and no visible hair anywhere on her body. Unlike me, who has to wear jeans and long sleeved shirts even during the hot humid summers in Chicago to cover up my gorilla limbs.

My argument got me nowhere if you don't count the trip to my room for an "attitude adjustment," (the seventh-grade version of time-out.) 😑

Fourth, ...

Forget fourth. Three's enough. Honestly, I could come up with about a hundred reasons why I don't want to move, but I'm running out of room on the page, plus I really have to pee. Until next time,

Willa

P.S. Don't expect XOXO or hearts. I'm not that kind of person.

March 2, 8:07 P.M.

Dear M,

There's something I really need to tell you about me. (Actually, there are a TON of things I need to tell you!)

I had a talk last night with my dad about this stupid diary, how I didn't think it would help me to sort out my feelings. Only, the thing is, when I said the word "feelings," it was like all of a sudden, I started to have them, (feelings, I mean) and I started crying like a total baby.

Eventually we got to the real cause of my recent ... I guess you could say — *depression* — regarding our move to California. He said, "Willa, are you afraid if we move you'll never have the chance of finding your birth mom?"

It's crazy, I know. Thinking that after almost

twelve years you're still in the area, and
someday I'd see you, maybe walking down the
street or in the produce aisle of the grocery
store, a woman who resembled me, only a super
pretty version, and that we'd instantly know
each other because of our strong genetic
connection.

You would cry and apologize like crazy for
leaving me and I'd forgive you. And then
because you felt so bad about ditching me, I'd
be able to convince you to become a home
wrecker and break up my dad's marriage to
Diane so he could marry you instead. The
three of us would become one big happy family
and live in the greater Chicago area. (Unlike
Diane and Olivia, who both will have gained a
hundred pounds and moved to Arkansas to
marry rodeo clowns. FYI: Olivia's would have to
be a shotgun wedding because Olivia's only
fifteen.)

Anyway, it was my dad who suggested I should write to YOU in my diary. And not in some boring old way like "Today I got an A on my math test," but to go back in time to the beginning of my life, or as far back as I can remember, and believe me that's pretty far. Seriously. I'm not kidding. It's sort of "my thing." (I'll tell you all about it in a minute. Get ready to have your socks knocked off.) I honestly can recall with perfect accuracy, every single day of my life since the day you left me at Children's Home — which is saying something, because I was only one at the time.

My dad says someday, like, after I'm eighteen and my records are unsealed, that I might be able to find you, (if you haven't found me first) and it will make things a lot easier if I just hand you this diary with the Cliff Notes version of my life instead of unloading a bunch of rocket-fire verbal vomit on you as soon as we meet.

So I agreed with my dad that I'd write the entries in this diary to you personally. As you can see above, I'm going to start them with "Dear M," and not Dear Mom, because Diane is a total snoop, and if she found the diary she might think I was writing to her. (As if!)

I have to warn you though, my life hasn't been all rainbows and puppies.

I'm not trying to make you feel bad or anything, but it's been pretty brutal. Especially the orphanage years before I got adopted by the Shisbey's.

I'll keep it short for now. Olivia's talons are scratching at the door, and she's screeching I used up all the hot water for my shower, so I'll write again tonight after she's asleep.

Willa

Special thanks to the amazing folks at Kevin & Amanda Fonts for Peas for allowing the use of their amazing doodles. To download the FREE doodles used in this book, go to www.kevinandamanda.com

The following fonts were used:

Pea Karen's Doodles
Pea Fruit Salad Doodles
Pea Bethany's Doodles
Pea Cookie's Doodles
Pea Deliah's Doodles
Pea Deva McQueen
Pea Family Joy Doodles
Pea Jiawei Doodles
Pea Jillybean's Doodles
Pea Lauren Doodles
Pea Panda's Doodles
Pea Kiki Doodles
Pea KT Doodles
Pea Stacy's Doodles
Pea Stacy's New Doodles
Pea Shelly Belley's Doodles
Pea Tisha's Doodles
Pea KT Puppy Love Doodles

Pssst… Willa has a secret.

Confessions of a Nerdy Girl Diary Series

Top Secret   Truth or Dare   Unlucky Thirteen
Diary #1   Diary #2   Diary #3
Available Now!   Coming Soon!   Coming Soon!

Go to
www.subscribepage.com/nerdygirlTopSecret to
get notifications on how to get your FREE copy
of *Confessions of a Nerdy Girl: TOP SECRET*, or to
www.NerdyGirlBooks.com for more info.

ABOUT THE AUTHOR

Linda Rey

Linda Rey lives in Orange County, CA with her husband and a dog named Dude. Her favorite color is green, but blue is a close second. She'd rather eat potato chips than ice cream, but give her a donut and she'll be your friend for life. Linda's favorite books as a child were *The Secret Garden*, *Charlotte's Web*, and anything by Judy Blume. To get cool FREE stuff and her latest Nerdy Girl Books, go to www.NerdyGirlBooks.com or sign up for her newsletter at www.subscribepage.com/nerdywordz. Or you can email her at linda@lindareybooks.com (And yes, that's her real email. Unless you don't have something nice to say, then no, it's not.)

Made in the USA
Columbia, SC
06 December 2017